Courage
to Be

Courage
to Be

Organised Gay Youth in England 1967-90

A HISTORY OF THE LONDON GAY TEENAGE GROUP
AND OTHER LESBIAN AND GAY YOUTH GROUPS

DR CLIFFORD WILLIAMS

The Book Guild Ltd

First published in Great Britain in 2021 by
The Book Guild Ltd
9 Priory Business Park
Wistow Road, Kibworth
Leicestershire, LE8 0RX
Freephone: 0800 999 2982
www.bookguild.co.uk
Email: info@bookguild.co.uk
Twitter: @bookguild

Typeset in 11pt Minion Pro

Printed and bound in the UK by TJ Books LTD, Padstow, Cornwall

ISBN 978 1913913 632

British Library Cataloguing in Publication Data.
A catalogue record for this book is available from the British Library.

Contents

List of images

PHOTO 1 Youth Services Information Project meeting attendees in Torrington Square, London, May 1975. Back row (left to right): Graham Wilkinson, Peter Impey, Bill George, x, David Green, David Armitage, Micky Gibberd, Simon Ives, John Shiers(?), Chris Bowden-Smith. Front row (left to right): Billy (Adam) Brown, Diana Purcell, Nettie Pollard, x, x, Oliver Merrington, Trevor Locke, Angela Needham. x = unknown (photograph courtesy of Trevor Locke, who also supplied most of the names of those he can recall in the photograph).

PHOTO 2 On Valentine's Day 1976, young people presented to the Home Secretary 1,000 letters calling for a reduction in the homosexual age of consent. Trevor Locke holding the file, Paul Welch with light beige jacket and furry brown collar and glasses, and next to Paul, Michael (with dark-framed glasses) (courtesy of Robert Workman archive, Bishopsgate Institute).

PHOTO 3 Left to right: Philip Cox, Gary James, Paul Welch, John Gill and Michael (possibly Imber) at London Waterloo Station. Philip, Paul, John and Michael were off to the CHE Conference in Southampton, 1976. Gary was seeing them off (from CHE *Youth News*, courtesy of CHE and LSE Hall Carpenter Archives: photo by author).

PHOTO 4 Trevor Locke (on left) and John Gill on stage at CHE Annual Conference in Southampton, 1976 (courtesy of Robert Workman archive, Bishopsgate Institute).

PHOTO 5 Philip Royston Lloyd Cox, born 3 October 1956, died 4 September 1992 (courtesy of Gary James).

PHOTO 6 Steve Power, 1977 (courtesy of Steve Power).

PHOTO 7 Robert Ian Halls, born 3 October 1958, died 27 February 1993 (courtesy of Robert Workman archive, Bishopsgate Institute).

PHOTO 8 Left to right: Keith (surname unknown), Peter Langford, Robert Halls and Neville Magee, upstairs at 296 Holloway Road on 17 April 1977 (courtesy of Robert Workman archive, Bishopsgate Institute).

PHOTO 9 LGTG day trip to Brighton, 1978 (courtesy of David Gough).

PHOTO 10 Tom Robinson at the LGTG, 1978 (courtesy of Steve Power).

PHOTO 11 Left to right: Steve, Shelia, Chris Heaume (with cigarette) and Uli at West Wittering, Sussex, April 1979 (photo by author).

PHOTO 12 Gay Youth Groups: guide produced by the Joint Council, December 1980 (photo by author).

PHOTO 13 Letter 26 September 1979 confirming the LGTG was registered as a youth club (courtesy of Steve Power, photo by author).

PHOTO 14 Manor Gardens Hall, where the LGTG met from 1979 (photo by author).

PHOTO 15 Del Campbell (on left) and Martin Collins in the office at Manor Gardens (courtesy of Gregg Blachford).

PHOTO 16 On the Huddersfield Gay Pride march in June 1981 the GYM banner was present (courtesy of Robert Workman Archive, Bishopsgate Institute).

PHOTO 17 Jane Skeats (on left) and Gilly Salvat (courtesy of Martin Collins).

PHOTO 18 Cover of LGTG Annual Report 1982 (photo by author).

PHOTO 19 Badges produced (photo by Gregg Blachford).

PHOTO 20 *Barriers* play by LGTG at GYM event, 27 March 1983. Left to right: Jain (Jane) Clarke, Carl Spurling and Steve Lunniss (courtesy of Robert Workman archive, Bishopsgate Institute).

PHOTO 21 Scarborough, 1983. Left to right: David Joad, x, Christopher Shoulder, Gavin Simmons, Gary Barker (courtesy of Martin Collins). X declined to be identified by name in the book but was happy for the photo to be published.

PHOTO 22 Andy (on left) and Jeff, taken for *Something to tell you.* Images of teenage boys kissing were rare then and still are outside of pornography (courtesy of Martin Collins).

PHOTO 23 *Something to tell you*, by Lorraine Trenchard and Hugh Warren, was published in 1984, followed by three more reports on youth work, young lesbians and school (photo by author).

PHOTO 24 LGTG placards at Gay Pride 1984 (courtesy of Robert Workman archive, Bishopsgate Institute).

PHOTO 25 Cover of *Visions* (courtesy of Gregg Blachford, photo by author).

PHOTO 26 London Gay Teenage Group outside the meeting hall in Manor Gardens, October 1984 (courtesy of Gregg Blachford).

PHOTO 27 London Gay Teenage Group outside the meeting hall in Manor Gardens, summer 1985 (courtesy of Gregg Blachford).

PHOTO 28 Author, 1981 (copyright author).

Acknowledgements

I should like to thank all those who shared their recollections of their time in the London Gay Teenage Group and other gay and lesbian youth groups. I hope the inclusion of their personal testimonies in this book will help readers to gain a sense of the real lives behind the history of organisations and movements that this book charts.

The assistance of staff at various archives has been invaluable. In particular Gillian Murphy at the London School of Economics Women's Library, and Stef Dickers at the Bishopsgate Institute Archives, have answered many of my questions and helped me find documents.

I am very grateful to those who kept documentation and ephemeral material relating to the London Gay Teenage Group and other early gay and lesbian youth groups. In particular Gregg Blachford, Steve Power, Maureen Hand, Jane Dixon, Steve Lunniss and Matthew Scudamore had kept important papers which I was able to examine.

Martin Collins set up a closed Facebook group for past members and this has provided an excellent forum for sharing old photos, memories and reconnecting with old friends.

Trevor Locke provided valuable insight and information into the work of the Campaign for Homosexual Equality Teenage Movement and Youth Information Services Project.

I am grateful to those who have allowed me to reproduce photographs. These are credited in the list of images.

Both Chris Heaume and James Byrne provided great assistance in reading through my drafts and suggesting changes. David Green carefully created the index. However, any mistakes left in the book are down to me.

Introduction

This book started out as a personal journey back to my youth. I grew up in a south London suburb and attended a comprehensive school. I had passed the 11+ examination to attend the local grammar school, but my father insisted all three of his sons attend the comprehensive. If I had gone to the grammar school I may have got to know Brian Paddick (now Lord Paddick). He went to that school and grew up in Sutton at the same time. We both possibly thought we were the only gay boys in town!

Certainly being gay at school in the 1970s was a lonely experience. Homosexuality was considered an illness and a sin. We were referred to as pansies, poofters and queers (then a term of abuse).[1] Of course it was impossible to 'come out' at school. I doubt I had even heard of the term. The only gay men I knew about were television personalities like Larry Grayson and John Inman. They represented the stereotypical queer: camp, effeminate and a figure of fun. There were no appropriate role models. And the law then made any gay sex illegal until both parties were 21 years old.

I had crushes on boys and had no interest in girls. I knew by the time I was 14 or 15 that it was the way I was. I just had to keep quiet about it and keep my fantasies to myself.

Some other boys suspected I was queer and called me a poof or bumboy. Often the boys that called me names like that were ones I fancied, and I hoped they might grab me and force me to do things with their bodies. That never happened, but I could at least imagine it.

After leaving school my quest for information about homosexuality led me to consult the few books available on the subject. There was no internet then. No mobile phones. Books and encyclopaedia entries usually referred to the mental illness and neurotic condition of homosexuality. Sometimes treatment or prayer were suggested. I read about aversion therapy.

It must have been in 1978 that I discovered *Gay News* and plucked up the courage to ask for it in the local library. Sutton Library was one of the few libraries bold enough to stock it.[2] But it was kept behind the counter. Asking to see it was tantamount to coming out! I read in *Gay News* that there was a London Gay Teenage Group. I don't think it was long before I sent them a letter asking for more details. I soon found out that they met on Sundays in Holloway Road, London, and were open to anyone up to the age of 21.

London was accessible. I knew the tube system. I most probably caught the bus to Morden, then the Northern Line, before changing onto the Piccadilly Line. Alighting at Holloway Road underground station one Sunday afternoon I made my way to number 296, above a chicken takeaway shop (!) called Theeba. I found about 20 young guys of my age and a couple of adults. I recall John Stevens, a pleasantly spoken young civil servant, speaking with me and making me feel welcome. I learned recently that he went on to become a youth worker and manager. Soon I was making friends, including Phil, a punk boy from south London whom I became a bit infatuated with.

The group was unique. There was no such group anywhere else in Britain at the time. London was a magnet for gay men, and the teenage group a safe haven for many young men and a few women. Gay at that time also meant lesbian, but the group never attracted many women. So in due course a separate young lesbian group was established. A few women did attend the LGTG quite regularly; I remember Shelia and Zoe.

Shelia came on the camping trip in April 1979 along with about 12 young men. Chris Heaume, youth worker and pioneer in the field of provision for gay teenagers, drove the minibus.

Chris also drove the minibus on some of our social outings, trips to places like Ipswich and Norwich, where in the evening we attended the local gay disco. There were no regulations to follow or forms to fill out or parental consent. We just went and questions were rarely asked about age on the door. I know some of the young men were under 18, but that did not stop them attending the discos and drinking alcohol.

Such trips led to some memorable nights! Crashing out at friends' houses or flats in London, sleeping on floors and enjoying gay sex for the first time! A liberating experience. But also the heartbreak of falling in love with people who were only interested in sex, and finding out that the gay scene seemed full of one-night stands and little love. It was a scene where sex was a commodity and quite segregated from emotional attachment.[3] This was all pre-AIDS. So for that I am grateful. But personally I found a lack of love, or any thought that you could have a fulfilling long-term relationship with someone of the same sex, and this led me to disillusion and despair. At that time there was no gay marriage or even a suggestion that such an idea would ever happen. That was pure fantasy.

I recall one upset: meeting a young man and having lovely times together and then not hearing from him for days and realising he was not in love with me like I was with him, then going out into the countryside with a big knife and contemplating slashing my wrists and ending it all.

Emotionally I was a wreck, but fortunately Chris Heaume put me in touch with a counsellor which might have saved my life. Although sometimes in the years since, when suffering from severe depression, I have wished I did commit suicide then. It would have saved all the anguish later in life.

Going to university and being good academically gave me a lifeline. I also began to be interested in women sexually. I came to the conclusion I was bisexual. That was more difficult than coming to terms with being gay. The gay communities thought of you as closeted or selling out! The straight communities might say things like 'being greedy' or 'you are really gay'. But it was clear to me that I was interested and enjoyed sex with both sexes, and that the person and their looks were more important than what was in their pants.

I have reflected on growing up and got involved in researching LGBT history. I started trying to find people I had lost all contact with. First Chris Heaume – easier with the internet and when someone's surname is less common. Chris still had some papers from the LGTG days. Then I found material in archives. Especially the Hall Carpenter Archives, where the late Micky Burbidge's papers were held. And then I met Steve Power, who still had loads of papers, including a piece I had written about our camping trip to Surrey! I established contact with Gregg Blachford in Canada. Gregg was the first paid part-time youth worker at the LGTG. He had a lot of photos (alas after my time at the group, but nevertheless a great resource). Soon Martin Collins had set up a Facebook group for old members. By this time I had established that the LGTG had folded sometime around the end of the 20th century.

Over Christmas 2018 a parcel arrived from Canada. It was exciting to open it and find all of Gregg's LGTG papers which he had agreed to donate to the Hall Carpenter Archives in the London School of Economics. I loved sorting through these papers, preparing catalogue entries for them and handing them over to the archive.

Oral histories and other retrospective memories often contain vague or inaccurate detail. There have been a number of occasions when people have related what they considered facts only to be faced with the documentary evidence to the contrary. Specific years and dates can often be recalled inaccurately. This is why I have relied heavily on the archive documentation, although some of that is undated. And of course the original printed material can be wrong! Do not believe everything you read in newspapers, for example. Once something gets into print, it is then sometimes reproduced over and over again, and inaccurate information can get embedded as 'fact' in history.

In February 2019 I was invited to talk at the LSE during LGBT History Month, sharing a stage with famous gay activists Lisa Power and Stuart Feather. The auditorium was packed for my presentation about 'the history of possibly the first gay teenage group in the world'. Later that month I also gave the talk in the National Maritime Museum, where Peter Scott-Presland was also talking [4]. Other talks followed (by Zoom when Covid struck).

Jane Dixon and Maureen Hand provided much information about the provision for young lesbians in 1980s and '90s London. This book includes their accounts of what was happening in Islington and Camden, and how the North London Line organisation stretched out to help many young people.

Trevor Locke helped with the story of how the Campaign for Homosexual Equality was involved in setting up the foundations of what became the LGTG. I am very grateful to those in CHE who so precisely recorded things and filed them, thus ensuring their archives would be useful for future generations.

It has been an absolute pleasure to conduct the research for this book. I love archives and discovering old documents and reports. I feel this is an important part of 'hidden history' to reveal. Many who were there all those years ago are sadly dead. Others need to record their recollections before it is too late. I thank those who have answered that appeal.

Clifford

Dr Clifford Williams
July 2021
Dis-United Kingdom

Abbreviations

AIDS	Acquired Immunity Deficiency Syndrome
BFI	British Film Institute
BL	British Library
CHE	Campaign for Homosexual Equality
CHETM	Campaign for Homosexual Equality Teenage Movement
FB	Facebook
GLC	Greater London Council
GLF	Gay Liberation Front
GN	Gay News
GYM	Gay Youth Movement
HCA	Hall Carpenter Archives
HIV	Human Immunodeficiency Virus
ILEA	Inner London Education Authority
JCGT	Joint Council for Gay Teenagers
LAGNA	Lesbian and Gay News Archive
LGBT	Lesbian, Gay, Bisexual, Transgender
LGTG	London Gay Teenage Group
LGYM	Lesbian and Gay Youth Movement
LL&GC	London Lesbian and Gay Centre
LLGTG	London Lesbian and Gay Teenage Group
LMA	London Metropolitan Archives
LSE	London School of Economics
NAYC	National Association of Youth Clubs
NCVYS	National Council for Voluntary Youth Service
NLL	North London Line

NUS	National Union of Students
NUSS	National Union of School Students
PIE	Paedophile Information Exchange
SAYS	Sexual Awareness in the Youth Service
TNA	The National Archives
YLG	Young Lesbian Group
YSIP	Youth Services Information Project

Chapter One

EARLY ROOTS. ALBANY TRUST, PARENTS ENQUIRY, CHE, GLF, AND PROVISION FOR YOUNG GAY PEOPLE, 1967-73

The use of the word gay for homosexual starts to appear in the UK in the 1960s. Before the establishment of common usage of the word with this meaning, gay was used to mean bright, cheerful. As such, there was a 'Gay Youth Centre' in Carlton, Nottingham in 1962,[5] and GAY was also the acronym of the Guild of Abstaining Youth.[6] These two examples are a warning to future historians not to rely on a word search as providing definite proof of the existence of something in the past, because in the past the word had a totally different meaning.

In 1968 a 19-year-old teenager, who lived on a council estate and worked as a clerk for a steel firm, featured in a full-page interview in the *Wolverhampton Express and Star*.[7] His name was John Holland (his full name was not given in the article). John told the reporter that the 1967 Act (which partially decriminalised homosexual acts) did not go far enough and that he was homosexual. He said 'The Act shows the community is at last beginning to accept us as human beings and realizing that we are not freaks or perverts'. John launched the Male and Female Homosexual Association of Britain (known as MANDFHAB). Holland prepared membership forms, had plans to raise money to purchase a club house and consulted the Albany Trust, a small but pioneering London-based psychosexual counselling organisation.

Antony Grey of the Albany Trust was horrified and thought the 19-year-old naive and a danger to CHE's plans to start up Esquire Clubs for those aged 21 and over. He thought this boy 'damp behind the ears',[8] and that he might bring homosexuals into disrepute and jeopardise the chances of The Campaign for Homosexual Equality (CHE) establishing clubs.[9] By the autumn of 1968

MANDFHAB had 'floundered'. Holland was overwhelmed by the volume of enquiries and his postage costs exceeded subscriptions.[10] Holland went on to set up a Wolverhampton CHE group which did admit anyone aged 16 or over. Scott-Presland (2015) remarks: 'The issue of whether to admit people between the ages of 16 and 21 was one which exercised many groups over the next few years, and could cause some controversy'.[11]

The Sexual Offences Act 1967 did not make legal any sexual activity between males, or with males, aged under 21 years old. Those who acted outside this law, and were caught, were sometimes dealt with harshly.

At Stafford Assize Court on 6 February 1968 a group of teenagers were convicted of homosexual offences. One was aged 16, two were 17 and the other was 19. The 19-year-old had organised parties in a flat. Three were sent to Borstal (young offenders' imprisonment with training). They appealed and two had probation orders substituted instead of Borstal training. Judge Lord Justice Winn said in the Court of Appeal that 'the conduct of these youths in itself not abnormal for young men of their age group, was wrong and disgraceful because parties were held to facilitate, if not stimulate, homosexual intimacy'.[12] Such harsh sentences for under-21-year-olds who committed consenting acts with persons over 16 were unusual. Those aged 16 to 21 years old were often cautioned as an alternative to court proceedings or if prosecuted they might be placed on probation. The law came down more severely on those aged over 21, especially if the other party was under 21. The wider the age gap the more severe the sentence generally.

ALBANY TRUST

The Albany Trust was founded in 1958 to promote psychological health through research, education and social action. It worked largely on the personal and social problems of homosexuality. It provided training and publications for those working with people experiencing personal or social difficulties because of their sexuality.

The Trust found itself dealing with the issue of adolescent males who identified as homosexual. A small supervised group meeting of under-21 youths was held in London (with two Samaritan volunteers present) in 1968. This was found to be beneficial, but some of the participants had such long journeys it seems the group was unable to meet regularly. This may have been the first group of its sort for young gay men under 21.

Correspondence from a youth in Sheffield led, in April 1969, to Antony Grey suggesting to David Hepworth, of the Public Health Department, the 'possibility of arranging some protected social meeting place for the younger people like "Y" who feel extremely isolated and not particularly enamoured of the known pubs etc in Sheffield'. David Hepworth's unencouraging response of 22 April 1969 stated that he had 'personal reservations and apprehensions about the possible effect on certain rather unstable adolescents... It still seems to me that there are dangers in such groups being too un-supervised, if only the risk of re-enforcing what are merely hetero-sexual inhibitions'.[13]

In suggesting such a group be set up in Sheffield, Albany Trust case worker Mrs C F (Doreen) Cordell (based in London) wrote to a Sheffield doctor in more supportive terms:

> We feel that if some of these young people are indeed to live their lives with a homosexual orientation they need much support, encouragement in the everyday things of life, career and families etc., and guidelines as to what a homosexual life can be like rather than the misconceptions that exist. So many of them come to us, knowing that this is what they are and despondent for what is ahead of them and, from my personal point of view as having been trained in youth welfare, I feel it is very important that they know there are many others who live healthy, constructive 'giving' lives, in the forefront of their chosen professions, in spite of the attitude of society in general to what they, through no fault of their own, happen to be. How can we bring a group of this kind about in safety to the boys concerned?[14]

Dr Orme replied by letting Mrs Cordell know he would discuss the issue with colleagues in psychiatric and social work circles. He also suggested the Sheffield Youth Development Council might be approached. 'It would obviously need some considerable degree of professional ability to carry out successfully the ideas you suggest'.[15] The Sheffield Youth Development Council were running a confidential counselling and advice service called 'Off the Record'. It is not known if any group for gay youth under 21 resulted from these discussions.

Parents Enquiry was set up in 1968 by Rose Robertson (1916–2011), a World War II veteran of the secret services (Special Operations Executive spy in France). Robertson writing in *Gay News* in 1977 said that she was quite appalled at the hypocrisy of a society which refused to accept that there was simply an alternative way of loving. The spur for getting involved was when she had two young men lodging in her house who were in a relationship that was outside the law.[16]

Based in Catford, south-east London, Rose set up a service for gay children (15–19-year-olds) and their parents. In 1973 a piece in *The Observer*, entitled 'If your child is queer', outlined the work of Parents Enquiry and the support they gave to parents and their children.[17] Later that year the *Sunday Times* also ran an article about Rose Robertson's service under the heading 'Help for effeminate boys' and referred to research by Bates and Bentler.[18]

Steve Power, who was chair of the London Gay Teenage Group from 1977–80, said that 'Rose was wonderful and she helped guide my thoughts. She was like a mum'.[19] She helped Steve through difficult times for the LGTG.

In 1974 *Gay News* reported that Parents Enquiry were hoping to establish a base in the borough of Kensington and Chelsea.[20]

Rose Robertson was a constant advocate and supporter of youth provision for gay teenagers. Her practical support and campaigning were a valuable part of the development of early provision for gay teenagers in Britain.

GLF (GAY LIBERATION FRONT)

A small number of gay (homosexual) youth groups existed in the 1970s in Britain. Research suggests the first was the Gay Liberation Front Youth Group, unless one counts the Albany Trust Group for under-21s in 1968. The GLF Youth Group was a loose-knit group and, like most of the GLF activity, was quite unstructured. It emerged in 1971 (the GLF itself having been set up in 1970). There was no formal organisation, but certain individuals galvanised activity. An undated leaflet of the Youth Group states:

> It exists to bring young gay people together to meet other young homosexuals to discuss action that can be taken to confront the many legal and social problems facing homosexuals under the age of 21.

Four demands are listed in the leaflet:

1. The Youth Group demands the reduction and eventual abolition of the age of homosexual consent.
2. The Youth Group demands complete unbiased sex education in schools, and in adult sex education literature.
3. The Youth Group demands that young homosexuals are not subjected to psychiatric avertion [sic] at school or work through their homosexuality.
4. The Youth Group demands an end to discrimination of young homosexuals at school and at work.

The leaflet also states that the Youth Group exists to promote discussion amongst its members, leading to an awareness group among young homosexuals. The leaflet ends with 'POWER TO THE PEOPLE!' in bold type.[21]

The Youth Group was largely run from a commune in Muswell Hill. Tony Reynolds was a key figure. Alaric Sumner (Power 1995) states that Tony Reynolds was the prime mover in the Youth Group and organised the events of summer 1971.[22] The Youth Group produced one edition of *Come Together* (issue 8), a newspaper from the GLF. Issue 6 also mentions the GLF Youth Group. Reynolds later worked for *Capital Gay*. Nettie Pollard recalls going to one meeting in Tufnell Park, in mid-1971, when the group were planning a demonstration and the youth issue of *Come Together*.[23]

Significantly the Youth Group led a demonstration march in August 1971 in London known as 'the age of consent march'. Some see this march as the first UK Pride event; others date the first UK Pride to 1972. The group also leafleted pubs, spoke in schools and stated that changing the age of consent was one of the aims of the group.[24]

The GLF Youth Group merged with the Education Group and thereafter was known as the Youth and Education Group.[25] The Youth and Education Group put together issue 14 of *Come Together*. In June 1972 they organised Gay Pride week.[26] Leeds (GLF) Broadsheet no 13 (January 1973) lists a contact address of 5 Martindale Road, London SW12 for the GLF Youth Group.[27]

In 1972 *Come Together* reports on a 17-year-old who was convicted of importuning at Victoria Railway Station (London) on 20 February 1972. The youth stated:

I went into the public convenience at Victoria Station for purely natural purposes. However whilst I was in there, I noticed a young man who appeared to be very interested in me and who I found rather fascinating. For reasons of pure curiosity, I found that I stayed there much longer than I originally intended, and realized my motives for being there could easily be interpreted the wrong way by the police. I subsequently decided to leave, and was on my way out when I was taken by the arm by a police officer at the bottom of the stairs. Since I came to the GLF I have made so many friends, I won't feel lonely any more; I wish I'd known about Gay Lib before.[28]

GLF was very active in the early 1970s but had divisions and factions within, much in-fighting and later fizzled out (Feather 2015). Its very radical activities would only appeal to a very small proportion of gay men and women. But there were offshoots from it. In 1973 a group called 'Icebreakers' was born out of a meeting of the Camden GLF.[29] 'Icebreakers' was a befriending service that continued into the 1980s.

In 1974 the South London GLF was still very active and established a gay community centre at 78 Railton Road, Brixton.[30] But generally the active life of the GLF was short, full of drama and of comparatively limited political significance. In recent years a rather romanticised version of the GLF has developed, creating the impression that it was more influential than other more sober, long-lasting and traditional political campaigns for equality.

Birmingham GLF produced a booklet, *Growing up homosexual*, which featured photographs of genitalia and advice on sex. The booklet was recommended in a publication by the National Association of Youth Clubs, but this brought some stinging criticism from some in youth work who felt the booklet was inappropriate for young people.[31]

STUDENT GAYSOCS

This book does not address the scope and development of Gay Society groups set up in universities and colleges. But clearly most students were teenagers when they first attended places of higher education. Some GaySocs catered for non-university and college young people, and events held in places of higher education were often important in the history of gay youth.

For example, a Young Gays Conference was held at the University of London on 24 June 1972, in University College. The event was organised by the University of London Homophile Society (GaySoc) and chaired by Robert Maynard, according to the report in *Gay News*.[32] The report also suggests it was mainly students who attended. Papers in the Hall Carpenter Archives (HCA) give details of other organisers involved. They state the event was organised by University College of London GaySoc and CHE London Youth Group, in association with the University of London GaySoc. Those attending could get into the evening disco at the Father Redcap for 10p instead of the usual admission price of 25p.[33]

The earliest GaySoc mentioned in Scott-Presland (2015) is the Manchester student group (Homophile Society) in 1969.[34]

The National Union of Students (NUS) played an important part in advancing campaigning for young gays. As Trevor Locke explained in 2020:

In April 1973, the NUS passed a gay rights policy motion at their Exeter conference. I would argue that if that student movement had not taken place when it did, the Campaign for Homosexual Equality's work on youth rights would not have happened when it did. Once the NUS had adopted a national policy of gay students, there was a movement towards young gay people generally claiming their rights. Soon after the NUS policy, CHE began to think seriously about its own young members and the status of young homosexuals in society. Had the NUS policy not happened in 1973, it might have been a much longer time before CHE turned its attention to the young gays campaign.

Once the NUS had a policy on gay rights there was a groundswell of work towards the establishment of gay societies across Britain's universities and colleges. Young people aged 18 to 20, began to think they should be part of the national homophile organisations. Young people's absence from the gay movement was no longer tolerated and taken for granted.

Most students were aged over 18. Even so, some secondary school pupils began to campaign for their rights within the parallel organisation – the National Union of School Students. CHE worked with that initiative although only from the outside. CHE focused its work on teachers and education more than on pupils.

Members of the CHE executive were impressed by what had been achieved in the NUS. They realised that it had much wider implications for both CHE and the British gay movement than just being something that happened within one organisation. CHE activists and officers alike began to appreciate that youth was an important issue, alongside many others. This fuelled CHE's commitment to lowering the age of consent from 21 to 18 (as some members would have it at that time).

Tens of thousands of students who saw what the NUS and the student movement was doing completed their education and went into work and society, taking with them a more liberal and progressive attitude to homosexuality than would have been the case in the absence of the student gay rights campaign. 1973 was a watershed year in the British gay rights movement and in public attitudes to homosexual love.[35]

The NUS motion instructed student unions throughout the country to help set up and finance gay societies. Jamie Gardiner, Gay Liberation leader from University College, London, who proposed the motion, said, 'Being homosexual is simply one of the many equally valid alternative ways of being a human being'.[36]

CHE (CAMPAIGN FOR HOMOSEXUAL EQUALITY)

CHE was born of out of the North-Western Homosexual Law Reform Committee (NWHLRC), which was founded in 1964 in Manchester by Allan Horsfall and Colin Harvey. NWHLRC became the Committee for Homosexual Equality in 1969. Committee was changed to Campaign in 1971.

The legal age of consent being 21 years (following the 1967 Sexual Offences Act), CHE was often nervous about the involvement of the organisation with young gay men under 21. Some CHE groups did not know what to do when young people under 21 turned up, and some groups felt so uneasy about this situation that they imposed a minimum age of 21 for group membership. Croydon CHE was one such group that did not admit under-21s.[37] Other groups appear to have been more relaxed. In the late 1960s two notable under-21 activists got involved in campaigning: Martin Stafford and Paul Temperton. Stafford was just 18 years old and doing his A levels when he first got involved in 1967 with the NWHLRC. The following year 19-year-old Temperton got involved and met Stafford. Temperton moved in with Stafford in the latter's parents' house.[38]

A Bristol CHE Youth Group existed in 1971–72, but it is believed that its members went up to age 26. Other gay youth groups that emerged also allowed young people up to the age of 25 or more. Scott-Presland (2015) lists a Kent youth group existing briefly in 1972.[39] A young CHE Manchester Group is listed in the GLF publication *Come Together* no 12 in spring 1972.[40] Scott-Presland (2015) refers to Manchester Young CHE arising out of the Manchester University Group founded by Martin Stafford.[41]

CHE London Youth Group started out as London CHE Group 5 in January 1971 and was open to people under 21, although it consisted mainly of people in their mid-20s. Group 5 were regulars at the Father Redcap pub in Camberwell.[42] They were renamed London Student Group before becoming CHE London Youth Group. Archived papers list Activities Secretaries in 1973–74 as Chris Butler and Andrew LeFevre, then in October 1974 Peter Impey.[43] Impey wrote to *Gay News* in 1975 pointing out that most members of CHE London Youth Group were in their 20s but that there was no minimum age for the group.[44] By 1975 the average age was 23. Out of 100 attendees only 14 were under 21. They had a vague upper-age limit of 25.[45]

In January 1972 CHE held its first youth conference in Manchester.[46] This attracted both CHE and GLF members.[47] In September 1973 at a CHE National Council meeting in Cardiff the Educational Campaign was launched. One impetus for this, previously mentioned, was the National Union of Students passing a gay rights motion. David Bell, a teacher and homosexual who had come out, was one of those said to have been particularly articulate in advocating the campaign. The CHE Educational Campaign was to be aimed at 14-year-olds to 19-year-olds. When headteachers did allow gay speakers to address pupils the CHE speakers were invariably asked, 'What do you do in bed?' One way of overcoming stereotypes was for four CHE members to attend the school (two women and two men). The campaign would help break down the misinformation about homosexuality as well as support gay pupils. The bulk of the campaign work would be done by local groups.[48]

The nervousness about involving under-21-year-olds in CHE was because of the fear of prosecution for 'conspiracy to corrupt public morals'. This was a common law charge that had been used by the state to prosecute organisations and publishers such as *International Times* and *Oz*. The 'offence' of conspiracy to corrupt public morals was established by the case Shaw v DPP (1961).[49] That case involved an appellant who had published a 'ladies directory' which listed contact details of prostitutes, the services they offered and nude pictures. He would charge the prostitutes a fee for inclusion and sell the directory for a fee. He was convicted of conspiracy to corrupt public morals, living on the earnings of prostitution and an offence under the Obscene Publications Act 1959. The appellant appealed on the grounds that no such offence of conspiracy to corrupt public morals existed. The appeal was dismissed. The House of Lords in effect created a new crime by case law.

International Times (*IT*) had advertising columns which were considered by the court to be obscene. At the trial in 1970 the director of *IT* was given a suspended prison sentence. CHE ran a correspondence club which enabled gay men to meet up with other gay men. CHE restricted membership of the correspondence club to those aged 21 or over because they feared prosecution if the club included younger men who might meet up as a result of the correspondence and commit illegal acts. The organisers of the correspondence club would then be liable to the conspiracy charge. This danger was also to hover over the London Gay Teenage Group in its early years.

Charting the relationship between CHE and under-21-year-olds shows how complicated this issue was. While Conference and Executive Committee could pass resolutions and policies, only local CHE groups could implement them and there was clearly some variation in the rules for different groups.[50]

In 1973 Liverpool CHE voted to admit under-21-year-olds and soon after Paul O'Grady, aged 17, went along.[51] Liverpool had established a youth group for 16-year-olds to 21-year-olds in March 1972 before the policy decision. This is the earliest evidence we have for a gay teenage group specifically for under-21-year-olds. And it seems the Liverpool police were quite relaxed about it.[52] According to Scott-Presland this group 're-amalgamated in February 1973' when Liverpool CHE lowered the minimum age of members to 16.[53] A few years later when the Joint Council for Gay Teenagers was set up in 1978, Liverpool was one of the first gay youth groups linked to it.

Chapter Two

HELLO YOUNG LOVERS: CHE YOUNG GAYS CAMPAIGN, 1974

In 1974 the issue of under-21-year-old males was debated at the annual CHE Conference in Malvern. The conference backed a motion to campaign for the lowering of the age of consent to 16. The Sexual Law Reform Society had called for the age of consent to be lowered to 14.[54] The CHE conference also called for support for Parents Enquiry. CHE member Trevor Locke argued for a youth campaign. A young gays campaign was established with a committee made up mostly of under-21s (the majority were under 18).[55] Details of the eight-point motion passed at Malvern can found in the CHE papers at the HCA.[56]

The editorial in *Gay News* (issue 49, 1974) was headed 'Hello Young Lovers' and went on to say:

…the anxiety and discomfiture experienced by the gay movement in dealing with this vexed problem is some indication of the strength of the social taboos, in fact, that it has been virtually impossible to discuss them at all… any adult advocating the reduction of the age of consent for gay men to 16 is accused of being a child molester, the automatic assumption being that that person is interested in reducing the age of consent for their own sexual gratification. If the person works with children… he is even more suspect. It is very difficult to take a stand on this subject without having one's motives suspected… Heterosexuals may consent at 16, therefore the same age should apply to homosexuals.

More encouraging though, is the motion CHE adopted to start a campaign for young homosexuals backed largely by the young gays concerned.

Trevor Locke recalled in 2020:

I went to London for the CHE activist conference at the University of London Union (ULU) [held on 20 July 1974]. I chaired the session about young gays. The first meeting of the CHE young gays committee was held at the London office of CHE [held on 25 August 1974]. Those present included me, Chris Bowden-Smith, Stuart Hunt, Rick Johnson, Alex Handford.[57]

That meeting of the Young Gays Campaign committee meeting on 25 August 1974 agreed that CHE youth groups should be limited to those under 21. The meeting also noted that the National Union of School Students (NUSS) had passed a motion supporting gay rights at their 1972 Conference and that they were trying to establish a group in London.[58]

At the Young Gays Campaign committee meeting held 24 November 1974 at CHE LIC (London Information Centre), Chris Butler proposed that a London Teenage Group be established under CHE (minute 56). However, 'the committee agreed that such a group could not be set up – even though there was great sympathy with the idea – but the way the committee felt for such a group to be established was to start it running under the umbrella of an existing youth club which was council approved and which would already be recognised by the community and official bodies'. At the same meeting there was a reference to a video tape film entitled 'The Criminal in Our Society' which was about the situation of the young gay in society (minute 54).[59]

At a committee meeting in Todmorden, Lancashire, on 8 December 1974, it was agreed to recommend to the executive committee the title be changed from the 'Young Gays Campaign' to the 'CHE Youth Services Information Project' (YSIP). This was because supportive organisations such as the National Association of Youth Clubs were less likely to work with groups with the word 'campaign' in them.[60]

The CHE Young Gays Campaign in December 1974 comprised of the following committee members: Trevor Locke (executive committee member and chair), Mike Gibberd (secretary), Alex Handford (treasurer), Richard Johnson (international liaison), David Armitage, Peter J Impey, Christopher J Bowden-Smith, David Dancer (NUS [National Union of Students] liaison), Graham Wilkinson (social services liaison), Sam Orrill (education and teachers liaison) and Dave Brown. Observers listed include Oliver J Merrington, John Morris, Rose Robertson, Tel Airs, Chris Butler, Simon del Nevo, Ian Everton, John Hudson, Veronica Pickles, Norman Redman and

Michael Trotter.[61]

In December 1974, 15-year-old Stuart Hunt, of the NUSS, spoke at the International Gay Rights Congress in Edinburgh and described being sent home from school for being gay.[62] *The Scotsman* reported that Stuart was suspended for 10 months from Cranford Comprehensive School, near Heathrow, London. He was told he was put on long-term sick leave after he declared himself to be a homosexual.[63] Sponsors of the Congress included David Steel MP, Gore Vidal, Iris Murdoch and Christopher Isherwood.

Of the main political parties, only the Liberal Party had any effective campaigning for gay rights within its membership. At their party conference, 20-year-old Richard Burden called for the age of consent to be reduced to 16 in line with heterosexuals.[64]

Chapter Three

In October 1975 the Albany Trust called a meeting at their offices in Clapham Road, London, to discuss the work being done in London to help gay teenagers at risk.[65] This followed the television programme *Johnny Go Home*, a documentary featuring the lives of young men and boys, like Johnny, who left home and arrived in London, prey to all the vices of the city.[66] Some of these young men were quickly recruited into prostitution and one, Billy McFee, known as 'Billy Two Tone', met his death during the production of the programme. Billy was found dead in a ditch in Sussex (featured in episode 2). The documentary was broadcast in July 1975, produced by Yorkshire TV.

For some gay teenage runaways, the prostitution business was one way to earn a living and have gay sex (but not usually with people they wanted to). Of course, many young male prostitutes who engaged in gay sex for money or other rewards were not necessarily gay or bisexual.

Harold Haywood and Antony Grey of the Albany Trust had a meeting with some senior officers of the Metropolitan Police to discuss young teenage runaways' involvement in gay sexual activity. Grey came away from the meeting 'with the clear message that the police regarded social workers and voluntary groups as ineffective and unimportant in the West End scene'.[67]

Johnny Go Home certainly brought the problem of runaway teenage boys and sexual exploitation to national attention. It also featured a 16-year-old girl who was using drugs and begging in the streets. The documentary focused in particular on the activities of a man called Roger Gleaves, who preyed on vulnerable young men and who had set up hostels for such runaways. At these hostels, Gleaves, who wore a welfare uniform and presented a respectable public front, abused several young people. Somehow he managed to get Thomas Wylie, the central character 'Johnny' in the documentary, onto his side. Gleaves' organisation had hostels in Lambeth, Hackney and its headquarters at 23 Drayton Park, Highbury.[68] Gleaves had previous convictions for assault against boys under 16. He seemed to operate with impunity.

When the police stopped and detained young boys, those who were (or pretended to be) over 16 were left to their own devices. Those detained under 17 had their parents contacted. In *Johnny Go Home*, a boy called Simon from Birmingham was interviewed and he described how he made money 'tossing men off', hanging around Playland (a games arcade near Piccadilly Circus).

After the documentary was broadcast the police mounted an operation at the Playland slot machines in Coventry Street, London. As a result five men were jailed, including Andrew Novac, aged 29, and Charles Hornby, aged 36, for their part in a boy prostitution racket.[69]

Problems with young runaways in central London had been raised by Bill Kirkpatrick, Richie McMullen (both of Centrepoint) and an ILEA youth worker in July 1974.[70] Their two page report points out that a large proportion (60–80%) of young males coming to the attention of Centrepoint, New Horizons and the Soho Project were involved in prostitution.

YOUTH SERVICE PROVISION FOR YOUNG GAYS

In 1975 the Department of Education and Science funded a post at the Albany Trust for a youth officer. Ric Rogers, who took up his post in July 1976, was the first youth officer before he went off to the National Youth Bureau. He was followed by Alan Smith in 1977.[71] A leaflet was produced called 'The Albany Trust, the Youth Service and the Psychosexual Health of Young People'. The leaflet outlined how the trust could help organisations in understanding sexual health issues, counselling and what sort of training programmes were offered by the trust.[72]

The National Council for Voluntary Youth Service produced a report in 1976 on young people and homosexuality. This reported on a working party that included Rev Neil Stedman, Tony White (Methodist Association of Youth Clubs), Sidney Bunt (National Association of Youth Clubs), Rev Eric Whitton (General Synod Church of England), together with co-opted Antony Grey (Albany Trust) and Marjorie Bryanton (probation officer).

It was the view of the working party that the needs of all young people, irrespective of their sexual orientation, should be met. The report stated that the Kinsey report findings were now 28 years old and 'yet only now is the existence of a sizeable segment of homosexual and bisexual men and women coming to be accepted'. The report stressed the importance of the quality of relationships, whether they be heterosexual or homosexual. They called for the training of professional and voluntary youth workers in sex education and greater awareness of homosexuality. 'Every opportunity should be made to communicate the message that homosexuality is no more and no less "natural" than heterosexuality'.[73]

After a couple of meetings hosted by the Albany Trust in the last quarter of 1975[74], Harold Haywood[75] and Antony Grey of the Albany Trust established a working party that convened in 1976. This group produced a report in April 1977 entitled 'Youth Service Provision for Young Homosexuals in Earl's Court'. The working party met six times and included Chris Heaume, Roland Jeffery and Ric Rogers (of the Albany Trust). It also included two representatives from Nucleus. Nucleus was an organisation which ran the Earl's Court Gay Help Service and whose reputation was later brought into disrepute by the activities of Charles Napier (sentenced to 13 years' imprisonment in 2014 for numerous sexual assaults on boys). The working party identified the need for youth services and a centre in Earl's Court, and produced some costings for such a centre. Legal advice was also obtained regarding any danger of working with young gay men under 21 where any gay sexual activity by those men would be illegal.[76]

The report noted the existing gay teenage groups in Manchester and North London (LGTG). In Appendix 2 Chris Heaume mentioned the 'CHE Teenage Group' weekly meetings at the Oval House Centre. So presumably his appendix report was written based on 1976 before the LGTG was meeting in North London. Chris Heaume also went on a four-day trip to Amsterdam, reporting back on provision for gay youth in that city.[77]

As Chris Heaume recalled of the Earl's Court project:

The vision was for a proper professional youth support venture. We were looking at premises which could have provided the right space for a gay youth venue, mixing entertainment (disco) and support functions, in a gay-friendly area. It was loosely named as 'H', Harold's nickname. The project took legal advice, but never materialised.[78]

Gay News reported on the CHE Young Gays Campaign (YSIP) in February 1975[79]. Trevor Locke had presented a report on the campaign which highlighted the need for more counselling support for young people and the precarious legal situation for helping young gays under 21. Trevor Locke also told the January meeting of the campaign that the vice-presidents of CHE were solidly behind a lowering of the age of consent to 16.[80]

Trevor Locke's report for the CHE executive committee dated 19 April 1975 discusses the issue of counselling for under-21s. He suggests a number of options: 1. Put all weight behind Parents Enquiry as main counselling service for young gays; 2. See that Friend is geared up to deal with young gays; 3. We call for or organise a new organisation to deal with those under 21.[81]

PLAN TO SET UP CHE LONDON TEENAGE GROUP:
FIRST SIGNS OF LONDON GAY TEENAGE GROUP IN CHE

On 2 July 1975 Trevor Locke wrote to the convener of the CHE London Youth Group. The letter acknowledges that the majority of members of the London Youth Group are in their 20s:

> If there is a large enough membership in your twenties age range then the formation of such a group would be a good idea if it keeps and attracts members into CHE. I do however think there should be a CHE based group for teenagers in London. I know there are other groups but I do not know much about them. Whether the teenage gay population is spread too thinly over them I do not know. The teenage CHE group, however, should be run by young people as far as possible.[82]

Trevor Locke then asked Pat O'Connor if he had enough teenagers in the London Youth Group to form such a group. In September 1975 Pat O'Connor wrote a brief report outlining that the London Youth Group now had most members in their 20s and was no longer a youth group as such. His proposal was to form a new youth group from the under-21s in the group, reform the current group but allow under-21s to continue or to join, and to provide an ongoing social and campaigning group for existing members. His plan would be discussed at the next meeting of the group at the University of London Union later in September.[83]

The London Youth Group subsequently was renamed CHE Young London Group (YLG), catering for those under 30. In September the following year CHE YLG were discussing the possibility of leaving CHE as CHE discussed 'de-recognising groups' [sic] with an age limit.[84] The YLG did however stay as part of CHE.

A meeting of organisers of under-21 gay groups had been held in London on 23 July 1975. The meeting requested CHE set up a group specifically for under-21-year-olds. Paul Welch said he would set up such a group.[85] It was noted that when CHE London Youth Group (YLG) was set up in 1971 members were under 21 but the average age was now 23 and of 100 members only 14 were now under 21.[86] A typical meeting might attract about 30 people of which four to eight were under 21.[87]

CHE YSIP Minutes of 15 August 1975 show Paul Welch as going to start the teenage group by meeting at CHE LIC (22 Great Windmill Street, London, W1V 7PH).[88] It was called the *Teenage Group* to make it clear it was for those under-21s only. This was the origin of the London Gay Teenage Group. CHE Young London Group (YLG) also used CHE LIC as a meeting place.[89]

CHE ANNUAL CONFERENCE SHEFFIELD IN AUGUST

The plan to start a teenage group was not something that the annual conference was happy with.

At the CHE Sheffield annual conference in August 1975 a majority of delegates rejected the proposals arising out of the 'Young Gays' workshop which had called for separate under-21 CHE groups and a separate Friend befriending service for young people. At the point of the motion being rejected, Trevor Locke tended his resignation from the executive committee. But an emergency motion was then passed supporting young people in CHE and Locke withdrew his resignation. Following this, 68-year-old Trevor Thomas and a 14-year-old delegate joined hands and raised them to celebrate the inclusion of the wide age range in the organisation.[90]

At the conference in Sheffield, there was tension generally between those men of a conservative outlook who attended as a social event and the activists (mainly women). The workshop held on 'Young Gays' discussed the problems of young homosexuals, the generation gap, young gays in our group (CHE), dangers of the law, possible actions for local groups and the way forward. The briefing document states, 'CHE national cannot attempt to recruit young gays if the local groups are not prepared to receive them'. One of the resolutions passed by the conference read, 'We should try to make adults in CHE groups aware of ageism and unconscious patronizing attitudes towards young people, local groups should avoid structures which are authoritarian and patronizing to young people. This will enable young people to fully participate in local groups'. However, the conference rejected a number of the proposals of the Young Gays workshop, such as a call to end the minimum age limit operated by some CHE local groups, as well as having separate youth meetings and a separate Friend unit for the young. Instead an emergency motion was passed: 'This Conference welcomes young people of whatever age and sex into CHE and asks the Executive Committee to talk to young people about how this may be done in a non-structured way'.[91]

The conference also supported a motion recognising the issue of paedophilia as part of the gay campaign and that 'an awareness of the sexuality of children is an essential part of the liberation of the young homosexual, and therefore essential to the young gays campaign of CHE' (an emergency motion proposed by Keith Hose and seconded by 11 people, most of whom today would probably be highly embarrassed to have been associated with this). The issue of paedophilia (sexual relations between adults and prepubescent children) was to haunt CHE and other gay movements throughout the next few years. Supporters of the Paedophile Information Exchange (which was forced to go underground a few years later when some of its members were prosecuted) managed to get into nearly all national gay organisations. Later they were to influence the Gay Youth Movement. Issues relating to the harm of paedophilia were downplayed at the time and the idea of debates such as those which took place at the CHE conference of 1975 taking place in the early 21st century are inconceivable. Paedophilia is nowadays one area of sexuality that is more or less taboo and certainly very strongly legislated against (more so than in the late 20th century, with laws relating to grooming being introduced in the Sexual Offences Act 2003).[92]

The recent report of the 'Allegations of child sexual abuse linked to Westminster' inquiry panel (2020) noted:

...the way in which the Paedophile Information Exchange (PIE) was able to gain support from certain civil society organisations for a period of several years. This appears to have been possible partly because PIE was not quite as open about its aims to begin with as it was later to become, and so its members were to some extent initially able to infiltrate civil libertarian and gay rights groups 'under the radar'. It was also because, as both Jeremy Clarke, a trustee of the Albany Trust, and Corey Stoughton, Advocacy Director of Liberty (formerly the National Council for Civil Liberties, NCCL), admitted, the governance structures and awareness of safeguarding in both the Albany Trust and the NCCL at the time were significantly more lax and underdeveloped than they are now.[93]

CHE TEENAGE MOVEMENT POST-SHEFFIELD CONFERENCE

The rejection by conference of the idea of separate CHE under-21 groups led to a rethinking by those involved in the teenage movement. Trevor Locke argued that the Youth Service Information Project (YSIP) had done useful work and carried credibility with youth organisations and should continue. He stressed that YSIP was not a campaign within CHE for young gays but a way of working with youth service organisations. Locke stated that there was a 'need for a new and unstructured campaign for young gays in CHE' (which would be separate from YSIP).[94] Young CHE members then met in London over the weekend 6–7 September 1975 and decided to drop the word gay from the title of the campaign and thus call it the CHE Teenage Movement. Tel Airs, aged 19, from Milton Keynes, would be the executive committee member for the movement.[95]

Gay News reported in October 1975 that two 19-year-old CHE delegates attending the National Association of Youth Clubs and British Youth Council Conference in Sheffield had been attacked in their bedroom by four hostile delegates. Colin Davies and John Grant sustained bruising.[96]

Teenage groups specifically for under-21s had by this time been established by the Campaign for Homosexuality in Manchester and London as part of CHE Teenage Movement. This was despite the idea having been rejected at the Sheffield Conference in August. The Teenage Movement was created as an internal campaign within CHE directed mainly at young people in the organisation. The movement's main objective was to improve the provision for gay men and women under 21 in CHE. Members of the TM Collective attended CHE groups giving ideas on how to encourage and support the under-21s. Alongside it CHE ran the YSIP, set up following debate at the CHE 1974 Annual Conference in Malvern[97]. YSIP was primarily aimed at dealing with youth service organisations rather than provision for young gays within CHE.

The YSIP cooperated with Oxford CHE in 'a highly successful conference on young homosexuals attended by many local teachers'.[98]

CHE Executive meeting of 16 November 1975 discussed the dangers of conspiracy charges. Minute 75/242 states that the 'Teenage Movement are subverting the wishes of Conference'. Alan C said starting teenage groups was against the conference wishes.[99] The year thus ended with a tension around the issue of under-21 gay teenagers and CHE. A tension that would lead to a split the following year.

Chapter Four

WE CAN DO IT OURSELVES: THE BREAK AWAY FROM CHE, 1976

In February 1976, on Valentine's Day, young people, organised by CHE, presented to the Home Secretary 1,000 letters, all from young people aged 16–21 years, petitioning to reduce the age of consent.[100] The Home Secretary's response was that he was asking the Policy Advisory Committee on Sexual Offences to look at the issue.[101] In essence Roy Jenkins (Home Secretary) felt it too soon after 1967 to change the law again.

YSIP started to produce *Youth News*, a bi-monthly newsletter circulated within the youth service. The first issue was December 1975 and was produced by Trevor Locke, Tel Airs, Tony Hancock and Mike Imber.[102] YSIP also ran a workshop at the NAYPCAS (National Association of Young People's Counselling and Advisory Services) Annual Conference. Trevor Locke, a member of the CHE executive committee, had responsibility for the social services campaign, as well as YSIP. Tel Airs, on the executive committee, had responsibility for the Teenage Movement. By the end of April 1976 Tel Airs had resigned. He felt that the Teenage Movement was being stifled by CHE. The national office told *Gay News*: He was asking for too much independence for the Teenage Movement.[103]

CHE Teenage Movement minutes of April 10th 1976 record that Tel Airs resigned. He had proposed CHE TM break away from CHE. This was not accepted by the meeting. Tony Hancock was elected in place of Tel Airs. Not long after this Tony Hancock resigned from his involvement in CHE TM (due to pressure of work) and John Gill took his place.[104]

CHE *Youth News* (vol 1 no 3) reported on the Teenage Movement meeting in London on 22 May 1976. John Gill, aged 19, 'who is to give the Teenage Movement Report to the Annual Conference at Southampton', reported that

'The London Teenage Group has since the end of last year, been operating under the aegis of Paul Welch, aged 18, and has unfailingly provided weekly activities for the group'. At that meeting it was noted that 'The caucus of CHE TM now appears to be in London, following the resignations of several leading members in other parts of the country. CHE TM sees its role... educating all people about young gays and trying to integrate teenagers into gay society whilst providing them with the opportunity to get together themselves'.[105]

The CHE Annual Conference at Southampton at the end of May 1976 agreed that local groups would no longer be able to operate age limits (e.g. only 21 years plus allowed to join). Conference also agreed that correspondents' lists should be open to under-21s. Legal adviser Ike Cowen told delegates of certain risks with this but that he was prepared to take them.

John Gill, of London N19, appeared on the stage at the Southampton Conference together with Trevor Locke. John also collated work for the publication of a book of poetry by young gay people.[106]

CHE Teenage Movement *Youth News* no 4, 1976, has a photo of a group of young gay men at London Waterloo Railway Station by the train (bound for Southampton) taking delegates to the CHE Annual Conference. They are named as Phil (Cox), Gary (James), Paul (Welch), John (Gill) and Michael (possibly Imber).[107] The front page has a report from the NAYC Annual Conference at the University of Birmingham which five teenagers from CHE attended. Jane, aged 17, says it was 'Really fant' [*sic*] and David, aged 16, says, 'We achieved a lot'. The NAYC conference called for an equal age of consent for homosexual and heterosexuals and equality for gay people. The motion by David Smith of CHE was passed 33–13. The CHE Tape slideshow 'Homosexuals in Society' was shown at a workshop where Trevor Locke spoke.

Ideas rejected at the Sheffield Conference in 1975 were now adopted as national policy. The report in *Youth News* on the Southampton CHE conference (May 28–31) says the 'youth motion sailed through'. The main youth motion urged CHE groups to arrange separate meetings for young people whilst still encouraging them to take part in the general group. It also noted the need to encourage more teenagers to join CHE. Another motion abolished the age limit on the members' correspondence list so all ages could now use this list. Age discrimination was also outlawed in CHE and groups that insisted on a minimum age could be rejected from CHE. The report notes, however, that 'Although conference is the sovereign policy making body for national CHE it is still up for the autonomous local groups to implement its policy... There is still some fear that allowing teenagers to participate might cause legal problems'. The report goes on to say, 'The teenage movement must now face the challenge of ensuring that these motions are implemented across the board'. On page seven it is reported that 'Paul Welch, age 18, convener of the London CHE Teenage Group has managed to start a gay society in the Greater London Council, where he works as a clerk'.

In the LGTG magazine *Metro*, in October 1978, Andrew Martin looks back at the start of the London Gay Teenage Group: 'We used London Friend's cramped offices and then equally cramped rooms at a place in The Oval before moving here [296 Holloway Road]'.[108]

The exact sequence of events in these early days of the London Gay Teenage Group may never be known. The key players are either dead or their whereabouts are unknown. Little was recorded, or if it was, the records have disappeared. The picture for 1976 is somewhat confusing. Different people recall events differently. We have fragments of information: places and names. What we lack is the precise details of what happened when.

Gary James, in his autobiography *Spangles, Glam, Gaywaves and Tubes* (2019), mentions attending a London Teenage Group meeting at the flat where Philip Cox and Paul Welch lived, near Old Street. James believes that this meeting, which was supposed to be all about rubber, was held in either autumn 1975 or spring 1976. He recalled that there were about 10 people at the meeting. His lift on the back of a motorbike to catch the last train to High Brooms Station, just outside Tunbridge Wells, from Charing Cross, is vividly described in his book.[109]

Youth worker Chris Heaume recalled:

I was asked in early 1976 by a youth worker in Earl's Court and a London Friend volunteer to meet with three young men at the Oval House cafe. They were trying to form a group and were looking for youth work support. It was suggested I could help as he was tied up as a full time worker, and I had left my job as the Warden of West Ham Youth Centre to freelance as an ILEA youth work trainer. The group of three tried for a couple of months in early 1976 to get a group together at the Oval House theatre, but the meeting room was far from the cafe [in the same building], so no-one came.[110]

Issue 4 of *Youth News* also reports that the London Teenage Group was to merge with an existing teenage group run by CHE's Friend, and that John Gill, age 19, had been co-opted onto the CHE Executive Committee.[111]

Friend was set up by CHE as a befriending service in 1971. It stood for Fellowship for the Relief of the Isolated and Emotionally in Need and Distress! Branches were established around the country. In 1975–6 Friend split from CHE. Around that time London Friend were based at 274 Upper Street, Islington. Steve Power states that London Friend had an under-25 youth group that met on Friday evenings. Some of the younger attenders at this group got together with the CHE under-21-year-olds who had met at the Oval and joined to form the LGTG.[112]

Funding for the move of Friend to Upper Street was provided by an Urban Aid Grant of £7,900, sponsored by the Borough of Islington and paid 25% by them, and 75% by the Home Office. One of the issues organisers had to deal with was the question of volunteers in Friend who used the opportunity of meeting shy young men, who were seeking assistance and information and friends, to go to bed with them. The topic was discussed at conferences as to whether it was ethical to bed enquirers. This issue divided many of the volunteers. As Scott-Presland (2015) states, 'It was a topic which brought disagreements between the male and female volunteers into sharp focus'. Many of the male volunteers thought it OK to have sex with clients.[113] Icebreakers was a similar set-up with less qualms about having sex with people who contacted it for company. The issue became a potential 'time bomb' for any gay teenage group.

In 1976 there were 25 Friend groups throughout the UK (including Northern Ireland). The booklet 'Introducing FRIEND in London' (1976) covered the potential problems of helping under-21-year-olds: 'Those who are under 21, and are male, present the particular difficulty of falling foul of the present legislation. Whereas the older isolated person can be introduced to a number of groups and so on. With younger people we have to be careful we are not suggesting a course of action which would be illegal'.[114]

The London Gay Teenage Group split away from CHE sometime in 1976. It is believed the Manchester group did the same. Despite the support at the national conference in Southampton (at the end of May), there was enough reluctance and caution in CHE for the brakes to be put on the development of a fully functioning gay teenage group.

As Steve Power (later to become the chair of the LGTG) recalled in 2019:

Philip [Cox] made it clear we would be wasting my time trying to pursue CHE support, as they were terrified of the legal ramifications of supporting under 21s ... The actual first LGTG facilitators and discussion of LGTG were held at a basement in Oval House, Kennington where several interested folk started to meet. Oval House played a key part in supporting the experimental theatre companies of the '60s and '70s, the emergence of gay and lesbian and women's theatre in the 1970s. These meetings at Oval House included Philip Cox, Paul Welch, Robert Halls, Andrew Martin, practically attempting to establish the outline for the group.[115]

CHE executive committee meeting minutes 21 August 1976 note 'John Gill wished it to be known that the teenage people in CHE wished to be called the "CHE Teenage Movement".[116]

In October 1976 CHE executive meeting minutes record:

The Teenage Group meeting in London was also causing Wallace [Grevatt] some concern as it appears to have broken away from the Young London Group. At Trevor Locke's suggestion it was agreed that the Executive Committee Campaign Group should discuss the position of Youth and Teenage groups generally and it was agreed to discuss the question at the next Executive Committee when (hopefully) John Gill will be present.[117]

The CHE Annual Report 1977 states that: 'We have refrained from taking any major initiatives in the youth services this year because we have been waiting the formation of the Gay Youth Workers' Group'. Trevor Locke had moved to a job in the National Youth Bureau in September (1976). The Teenage Movement had been dropped and Tel Airs had left.[118] CHE sought legal advice.

The governing body of CHE appears to have got concerned about the dangers to the organisation of provision for under-21 males. Under-21 females (not that there were too many women in CHE) were not an issue as no legislation prohibited lesbian sexual activity for teenagers aged 16 or over. CHE also might have felt that they had already got their fingers burnt by being too closely associated with PIE! Steve Power recalls that 'Philip [Cox] told Paul [Welch] to leave, he also told me that CHE were a waste of space'... The issue I think was a legal one, that they felt vulnerable to possible prosecution'.[119]

While CHE got cold feet, those young people involved in their London Teenage Group decided to break away and run the group independently. Although no concrete evidence exists for exactly when this decision was made, the split or break away appears to have come about in the autumn of 1976.

According to Andrew Martin, Paul Welch and Robert Halls were closely involved in running the group in the early days. 'They had practically set it up in late 1976… Paul left early on'.[120]

GRAPEVINE SUPPORT AND HOW THE LGTG GOT TO HOLLOWAY ROAD

By the autumn of 1976 Philip Cox had met with Richard Byrne, a pioneer of the world's first Young People's Sex Education Drop-in, and secured Grapevine's premises on a trial basis as a meeting place for the LGTG. Steve Power went on to work with Richard at Grapevine in Holloway Road.[121]

Simon Basler and Steve Power recalled how they first got involved with Philip Cox and the London Gay Teenage Group:

Meeting in Chadwell Heath during Steve's weekend break from college, Simon and Steve were going for a drink on a rather cold day. Simon was late and Steve called Simon's home, his mother said he had already left. In the phone box was a sticker for Gay Switchboard on the inside window. I showed Simon when he arrived as we huddled together in the red phone box. Simon and I went to the Coopers Arms Public House and discussed if we should ring the number, after a stiff drink we decided to call. I was 18 and Simon was 19 … The call to London Gay Switchboard in Nov 1976 started contact with Philip Cox on the switchboard. Philip explained that he had just secured the use of premises at Holloway Rd for a group for under 21s, and would we like to attend. He explained he wasn't supposed to use Switchboard to refer a young person under 21 to a group, but he decided he would, and said not to tell anyone. Philip was in training to become a switchboard member.[122]

Steve Power further recalled:

I attended the newly formed LGTG at the new premises [Holloway Road] with Simon Basler. I went into the 6th form and then left school in July '76. After school in 1976 I went to art college, I had just seen the film *[A] Bigger Splash* in Piccadilly with my art student friends, a David Hockney film shown in Piccadilly. Although I had already come out at school to four friends, the film prompted me to want to explore my sexuality more. Simon's age was 1 year older than me and he left the group at the end of May '79 at the end of his 21st birthday, so he was 19 at the time whilst I was 18.[123]

In October 1976 the National Council for Voluntary Youth Service published a 10-page report of their working party on 'Young people and homosexuality'.[124]

Steve Power recalls that in November or December 1976, a number of LGTG friends visited the Royal Court Theatre to see Gary James perform. Attendees were Chris Minter, Steve Power, Philip Cox, Robert Halls, Simon Basler, Andrew Martin and others.

Philip [Cox] left LGTG after the first meeting as he was 21.[125] He left a big gap. But [he] request[ed] that a number of folk put forward their names to run the group. Robert Halls was already there and overseeing secretarial duties and Andrew Martin publicity as original members. Andrew gets disgruntled that as the group moves forward young people have a democratic say but are ungrateful to those who helped establish the group.[126]

PHILIP COX

Philip Cox was born in Tiddington, near Stratford-on-Avon, 3 October 1956. His family moved around a lot with his father working in the aircraft industry. In the 1960s the family spent four years in USA. After his father left the aircraft industry his parents took over running the Blue Boar public house in Chipping Norton, Oxfordshire. It was here that Philip came out to his sibling, and here that his father discovered that Philip was reading books about homosexuality. Philip was taken by his father to the doctors to try and cure him.

Philip had a passion for radio, he listened to a lot of pirate radio and made friends with a disc jockey who was on Radio North Sea International. He went out on their boat on several occasions.

Philip left Chipping Norton for London when he was about 18 years old. He lived in a block of flats in Bath Street, near Old Street.[127]

In a radio broadcast, recorded in January 1983, Philip spoke of living in the USA when he was ten years old, playing with his friend Larry and sunbathing in the nude. He went on to describe when he moved to London and how flamboyant his flatmate was. Philip started wearing gay badges and got called 'queer' and 'poof' in the streets. He described how he was attacked in the street, along with his lover Neil, in 1982.[128]

Steve Power recalled more about Philip Cox and the early days at Grapevine:

Indeed Philip was an activist. Philip was a torch bearer for gay rights, he would often be seen writing Gay Switchboard numbers in public places,[129] he would read *Gay News* and follow up issues that he felt concerned about. He would attend gay rights meetings and call for action if required. Robert [Halls], Andy [Martin][130] and I did similar things, mine was pushing other organizations and networking, creating a support structure for newbies and pushing for money.

Philip in the few months I knew him was a quiet kind of a guy, not a big pushy one. He was strong minded but gentle. On a personal note I found Philip a little lacking in empathy and emotion, he often came across as cold and uncaring. Simon [Basler] went out with him and Simon has often told me that Philip was devoid of human emotions, especially when being intimate. It fitted. I guess he found a way of managing the damage sustained in childhood and his teenage years, by cutting off his emotional connections. He certainly was a somewhat cold character. Philip had the view the teenage group should always be run by under 21s and I promised him that if I was elected I'd ensure that agenda. Robert didn't like that idea, he tended to subscribe to the idea that those who put the concept together should run it regardless. But Philip was over 21 and Robert fast approaching. I was never sure about Andrew Martin at first but he tolerated the committee concept, critical at times, but put huge efforts into the support work for newbies we created. We relied upon honesty amongst us. So Philip left. Gary [James] recalls the reasons Philip gave when he asked Philip why give away your baby? Philip wanted to pursue new ventures, he was bored. Philip was no good at maintenance stuff. He was a creator. I was okay at doing both and so folk saw me as a potentially good organiser and front runner. I spoke my mind but was always careful not to exclude folk in the way I spoke.

At first, I was bloody angry at Philip for dumping everything and walking away. Paul [Welch] went within a week or so. It was a nightmare. Robert played a low-key back room admin role but was a rock, he would get letters out, and print materials. Andrew Martin was livid with Philip for putting up the concept of a 'members' vote on key roles. I think Andy always preferred the meandering group style and not putting folk in charge. Andy helped stop the group floundering a fair bit, he would ensure folk were spoken to, have a coffee made for anyone new and ensure discussions were had and music was playing. With few folk attending, and often losing new folk within a week of first arriving, we needed to ensure we gave as much as we could to help new folk arriving. Within weeks we had leaflets, stickers, headed paper, a book club, meet and greets at the station, a pen pal scheme for letters arriving to the BM Box and contacts with all the other key gay organisations. I met with Richard at Grapevine to ensure they continued their support. We were using their electricity and phones but had no way of paying. We set up a Sunday contributions coffee fund, and wrote for freebies and money to charities. There were few support processes in place for anyone attending, nothing really thought through, other than a record player, tea, coffee and biscuits and pushing for adverts in *Gay News* or other publications to bring in new folk. The group needed people, organising, it needed direction with a new sense of purpose and it needed money. And so the journey began in the winter of '76 to launch again in early February. I asked Philip for advice on a few occasions and he just reassured me I'd work it out myself! He was gone and wanted to pursue his radio work in Bath Street. I got on with just doing what needed to be done. However, I soon realised the bigger agendas and decided to network, go to gay political meetings, befriend the supportive folk and push those who sat on the fence to get their fingers out. The plan to meet politicians was a concept Rose Robertson and I worked on when opportunities arose. We scoured the press for articles, key contacts of our likely allies and made lists. Meanwhile the maintenance role continued. We did client telephone training with Grapevine, we met with VD clinics and health agencies, we worked with overseas contacts and tried to ensure we kept within the law of no under age sex on the premises. There is so much more to write about the logistics and projects we developed from the small beginnings. But I forgave Philip and realised he did his bit he was good at, challenging those to support a concept, which after he left we put into reality.[131]

Chapter Five

LONDON GAY TEENAGE GROUP FIRMLY ESTABLISHED, 1977-1978

According to *Gay News* the first meeting at 296 Holloway Road, London N7 was Sunday 13 February 1977 between 3–6pm.[132] Steve Power has stated that the group actually met there from December 1976, but publicity was sent to *Gay News* to state February as a safety measure. Mike Heary and Paul were given as contacts. These names were fictitious, but the telephone number was real. Later contact names were Mike/Carol.

Steve Power recalled being elected as chair:

The first young people's committee was formed in January 1977.[133] A ballot was undertaken with names in a box, I was elected as 1st young chairperson to run LGTG in Jan 1977, I promised I would stand and uphold the 21 rule. Robert [Halls] continued as Secretary and Andrew Martin was Publicity, Paul Welch was Treasurer I believe, but didn't last a few weeks before leaving, maybe he was 21 like Phil [Cox]?[134]

Paul Welch went on to be part of CHE Young London. In 1981 he was speaker secretary and Mike Imber was convener.[135]

Steve Power:

Our initial advertising resulted in a few letters and we gave these out to group members ... Time passed quickly. We discussed applying for funds and we got Andrew to start work on publicity. Robert did a quick survey of what members wanted. We produced stickers for placing our number around telephone boxes, etc ... Robert Halls was around during most of 77 but kind of came and went, on and off. We discussed writing to charities for funding and doing some fundraising events. Robert sent out letters.[136]

Steve Power developed a pen pal scheme as a response to the ever-increasing number of letters to the group. One lonely teenage boy living in Haverhill, Suffolk, wrote to the group and corresponded with Steve Power. Martin Willis is still in contact with Steve today and now living with his partner in France. In 2020 Martin Willis recalled his contact with the group by post:

Although I was born in London, I grew up in a grey, non-descript overspill town in Suffolk. I recall seeing Bronski Beat's video[137] and I could immediately relate to it. That was me, with a father who disapproved of everything that I was, the way I spoke, the way I wanted to dress, my tastes in music and who I wanted to spend my time with. I knew I was gay from a very early age. I knew that I liked other boys and that I wanted to have sexual encounters with them. In a hostile environment, having a gay penfriend was a glimmer of hope. I could write freely about my feelings with a like-minded boy who was experiencing the same pressure and rejection that I had felt for years. I had an older brother who fulfilled all the requirements of a normal lad; he liked football, girls and all the other trappings that that role entailed. So I always felt at a disadvantage, like I was inadequate and a huge disappointment and embarrassment for my father. Robert, my penfriend was very sympathetic and we exchanged confidences for a short time. It certainly helped until I was free to fulfil my own identity and express my sexuality.[138]

According to listings in *Gay News*, Icebreakers also ran an under-21s group.[139] The Icebreakers under-21 group may have started in May 1975. There are few archive references that have been found referring to an under-21 group of Icebreakers. The author has seen an entry in the Gay Switchboard logbooks (20 May 1975) referring to 'Icebreakers Youth Group for any gay person under 21 meeting every other Friday; Phone Tony or Billy on Icebreakers usual number 01-274-9590 for details, starting 30 May'.[140] On 15 August 1975 Billy Brown is shown as representing the Icebreakers Youth Group at the CHE YSIP meeting in London. Maybe the Icebreakers under-21 Youth Group folded once the LGTG was established?

Around April 1977 two members of the LGTG went to an Ipswich Youth Club, with Ric Rogers and Chris Heaume, and talked about being a gay teenager.[141]

The LGTG was featured in *Gay News* in May 1977 in an article entitled 'How we found out about sex'. A photo showed Keith (Ferris?), age 18, Peter (Langford), age 16, Robert (Halls), age 18, and Neville Magee, age 19 (the only one in the article whose surname is printed and who states he is 'bisexual actually'), sitting on the floor looking towards the photographer, who was Bob Workman.[142] Along with Gordon, age 20, and Trevor, age 18 (possibly pseudonyms), each give their personal accounts of how they were taught sex education. Sex was rarely discussed by any of their parents and Trevor remarks, 'My father does not speak to me at all now since he found out I am gay'. Gordon's mother told him, 'If I had a son like that I would smother him to death!' Robert admits going cottaging. He reads a lot, including Isherwood. Trevor stated he finds the gay scene frightening and unfriendly. He is also frightened of VD [venereal disease] and he wants a boyfriend. The article goes on to quote youth worker Chris Heaume, age 27: 'The first positive thing I saw on homosexuality was a piece of graffiti on a lavatory wall when I was 16.'

In the same feature Richard Byrne of Grapevine, who was based at 296 Holloway Road, talks about the sex education service they provided and described the organisation as a 'very unpressured and ambisextrous place'. The Grapevine office covered the two boroughs of Islington and Camden and provided sex education to schools as well as those who might deliver sex education. Claire Usher and Richard Byrne were the two full-time staff at the time of the article. Ric Rogers of the Albany Trust is also featured. He was appointed as the Trust youth officer in 1976 'to try and break the blockade against information on adolescent sexuality and sexual minorities in teacher training colleges and local authority training schemes for volunteer youth workers'. CHE's Trevor Locke refers to a new publication they are producing called *The Ambisexual Universe*, written by Michael Tovey and aimed at 15–18-year-olds. The publication challenges stereotyping of gays.

The developments in the Albany Trust, Grapevine and other organisations, in providing greater support for homosexuality as an acceptable status for young people, was not without opposition. Many people were alarmed by such developments. The Responsible Society held a meeting at the Department of Education in September 1977. They voiced their concerns about the Albany Trust, CHE, the Family Planning Association and the National Youth Bureau. They objected to government funding for such bodies being used to promote sex education which included homosexuality as something other than a problem and illness.[143]

The first June edition of *Gay News* carried an appeal by the LGTG for a record player.[144]

One of the first documents produced by the LGTG is a report 'The London Gay Teenage Group – a report after the first six months' (July 1977).[145] This gives the month for the group starting as January 1977 but mentions preparatory work in 1976. The report describes the meetings on Sunday afternoons 'in premises lent by a youth organisation in Islington [Grapevine], where two lounges, an office and a kitchen are available. The atmosphere is informal, activities include listening to records, playing darts, reading, chatting and discussing. Weekday activities have included discussions in members' homes, day trips to the seaside, outings to London discos, boating in Battersea Park, and so on … The age range of the group is wide from 14 to 20. The dominant age fluctuates, but is probably about 17 or 18'.

Steve Power recalled in 2019: 'We undertook trips out, did some raffles, played music, established a meeting policy for the young people arriving at the underground station, played educational films available at Grapevine'.[146]

The LGTG was run by the young people themselves with minimal adult assistance. This makes its survival and success all the more remarkable. Chris Heaume, as a volunteer adult and professional youth worker, helped with guidance, personal support, practical support (driving the minibus was invaluable) and, crucially, links with the authorities, national bodies, etc., to ensure advocates, supporters and eventually funders. But it was the members who ran the group, even when the first part-time paid youth worker was appointed.

Steve Power commented in 2020:

One of the most important things to grasp in our history is we were young people run, we listened to the adults who tried to help, or to those who gave ideas, but we often dismissed the ideas and even the adults involved! We trusted few adults as they all had their own agendas and often didn't understand or want to understand that being 'youth led' was the most important thing to us!

Many youth workers and heads of organisations used to get frustrated with us, we just sidelined them! Youth workers I'm sure found it hard to break into gaining our trust. Chris Heaume did a softly softly approach and won our confidence eventually. He was in tune with the concept of youth led and youth empowerment.[147]

Chris Heaume in 2018, remarked that, 'It is really nice to recall all that hard and good work we did. It really was a thorough grounding of a new sector in youth work, with the youth-led groups, the national push, the link to authority and status, the gradual civil affiliation and then funding, the research, the marketing, and so on'.[148]

From time to time members of the LGTG visited other youth clubs and spoke about being gay, trying to break down stereotypes and educating young people. Steve Power recounts one such visit that left an impression on several young people:

The one that stood out from many in the very early days was the Albemarle Youth House visit. It was a cold autumn night and we took the minibus to the outskirts of London/Essex Borders. Richard Larkins was the Senior Youth Worker, he had been working on a range of sex education work with his club. He had requested a session on sexuality and being lesbian or gay. We duly obliged. We arrived at what was a place full of teenagers, it was an edgy atmosphere and many young males were outside whilst the large percentage of girls were inside. The lads from the club looked at us with what I can only describe as fear and I can assure you we felt a similar fear about them.

There was a tiered seating system in a big hall and we were on the floor in front of the audience, there were few lads inside when we started. Richard introduces the session and the girls had a few simple questions pre-prepared. Once we got going the boys started to drift in and were hanging around the sides of the seating area or against walls. I honestly thought this night we were heading for a big fight! They looked daggers at us but some had cheeky smiles. One lad then shouted out a question when Richard asked if there were any more – 'Do you put a dick up your arses [sic]' – and laughter burst out everywhere. John Stevens bravely replied to this banter by shouting back, 'Yes, they stick it right in me, perhaps you could try it, you may like it!" The boy blushed, the girls laughed, other boys egging him on to make a date with John! It was hilarious! We then had what I can only describe as the most amazing frank discussion about gay sex and straight sex I think I have ever encountered. Royce evened up the debate with a question to the club members about straight sex. He said something like, 'If one of you girls are on a period do you still have sex and does

35

it get all bloody?' The girls, aghast, shouted, 'That's just gross no way I'm doing it if I'm bleeding!' The boys were in fits on the floor talking about jam and stuff. We learnt a great deal from each other that night. We learnt that even the hardest Essex lads and girls were inquisitive and open enough to discuss things, we learnt to hold our heads high and be who we were. We learnt that we could do this stuff ourselves with no major adult interventions. When we were leaving some of the lads outside said goodbye with banter like 'bye bum boys', our crowd replied by waving and shouting out, 'There's room in the back if you want a ride.' They were in stitches. I recall one of the lads in discussion with us after the event. He said, 'Some of you don't look gay, you can't tell.' One of our group said, 'Yeah, maybe your mate could be gay and you'd never know.'

Well, it was about a month after we had a letter from a boy at that club, he used a made-up name and said he was there that night. We offered a pen pal who wrote to him at the club for many months. Amazing times.[149]

In January 2019 Tigger recalled their first visit to the LGTG:

It was September 18th 1977, it was a Sunday afternoon. After walking up and down for over an hour to build my courage to go in, I climbed the stairs at Holloway Rd. I felt sick with nerves that disappeared the moment I arrived. I was 18. In the early summer of '77 there was a documentary called *Gay Life*,[150] ITV I think. It was talking about the seemingly larger numbers of gay people and the age of consent, it gave out the number of Switchboard. There had been other avenues available such as Campaign for Homosexual Equality, Glassbreakers [*sic*] [Icebreakers], Grapevine. And now for the under age youth a place to socialise, something that was more than country dancing in your village but not Heaven disco. There were so many other things that happened that year that anchors it to my memory, Elvis, Maria Callas, and Marc Bolan, the year I lost my cherry among other things. And I seem to remember that the group wasn't very long started.[151]

A bottle party was organised for Saturday 24 September 1977 – 'phone Robert [Halls] for details and bring plenty of booze!'[152]

Gay News 22 September 1977 lists the Manchester Gay Teenagers Group as meeting Tuesdays at 7.30pm at The Squot [*sic*], near University Theatre, Devas Street, off Oxford Rd. Telephone John or Stephanie 061-480-4187. It is possible that the Manchester Teenage Group was registered with the Greater Manchester Youth Association in 1977, making it probably the first gay teenage group to achieve such a recognition.[153] No records of the Manchester Teenage Group were found by the author in the Manchester City Library archives.[154] The Greater Manchester Youth Association existed as a registered company from 1978–2001.

WHO WILL BE MY VALENTINE?

Robert Gibbs was a 15-year-old Surbiton (London) schoolboy when on Valentine's Day in 1977 he felt very left out as classmates opened Valentine cards. He thought, 'I am never going to be able to send cards like that.' He went to a telephone kiosk and thumbed through the heavy, thick directory looking for the word homosexual. Finding an entry 'Homosexual – Campaign for Equality' and a telephone number, he rang and spoke to someone who was not helpful at all. Robert told the person that he wanted to see a man's naked body and was advised to go and look at statues in a museum! A few days later Robert rang again and this time he was more usefully given a telephone number for 'Friend', the CHE counselling service. After ringing 'Friend' he was invited to visit their premises in Upper Street, London.

Arriving at 'Friend' he found a lot of older men and had a chat with them. They told Robert about Grapevine and the London Gay Teenage Group and gave him another telephone number to ring. After ringing Grapevine, arrangements were made to meet a member of the LGTG at Kew Gardens (a convenient bus ride from Robert's home). Robert subsequently met Mike Salina and they had a chat whilst walking round a park. Robert was not sure what might happen but asked Mike if he was going to take him behind some bushes. Mike made it clear that was not what he was there for; it was just to chat and ensure Robert was a genuine gay teenager and not a queer basher or paedophile. Mike gave Robert details of the group, but for a while Robert was not able to get up to Holloway Road where the group met, so he rang the group and another person answered and said he would meet Robert (again at Kew Gardens). So before he ever got to the group meetings in Holloway Road, Robert was 'vetted' twice. Although he was later to learn that this second meeting should never have happened, and that on meeting this other person it was sex that they wanted. They got Robert back to their flat in Camberwell for a chat but then seduced him. This person Robert states was an adult helper who had been involved in work for Parents Enquiry[155].

Robert eventually travelled up to Holloway Road and attended the group. He told Tigger about his experiences and Tigger told him to report what had happened to the office. They said that should not have happened. The person in question was not seen at the LGTG again. And the LGTG introduced a system whereby two members together would meet any new enquirers.[156]

This incident of an adult having sex with a teenager who had made contact with one of the gay counselling support organisations was not an isolated case. Adults who abused their positions like this not only jeopardised the support structure but also the whole issue of public support for the advancement of gay rights. In addition they risked the law courts. There was no mention of safeguarding then but the issue was to crop up again when the Joint Council for Gay Teenagers (JCGT) came into existence in 1980 (anyone affected can still report abuse issues today if they were under 16 when any sexual conduct took place or, if over 16, the sex was forced upon them).

As a pioneering youth group, operating under the legal age of consent, it was important for the LGTG to be above question without being cold or restricting, to be seen to operate professionally, and to have trusted relationships with the authorities, with supporters and with its members.

The gay scene was very predatory and sex-dominated. One-night stands and promiscuity were so common that this was what many young gay people learned to be the expectation of being gay. And many went on to copy or practise that lifestyle. This meant that some older teenagers at the LGTG could be quite predatory at the group.

Michael Connew recalls an occasion when this was demonstrated:

I have been giving thought to an incident that happened at the group in around 1977–78. I have often thought that at the time I could have done more and think of the incident often. I joined the Teenage Group when I was 19 around March/April 1977. I religiously went most weekends to Holloway Road but after the fire and the move to Manor Gardens my attendance dropped. In fact I was a member till after I was 21. I remember talking about this to Chris Heaume and he said I could continue going because as I was 'a stabilising influence on the youngsters'. One Sunday in late 1977 a young boy turned up, he was 15–16ish (I shall call him John). I clearly remember being envious of him because he had already come to terms with being gay and was secure in his mindset. He wanted to meet other gays, he wanted support and friendship. He had found out about the group from Gay Switchboard and I remember a group of us sitting round listening to his story totally riveted and thinking afterwards this is what the group was all about. John was at a private/grammar school and obviously came from a well-to-do family. He and his best friend had had sex (in the school toilets if my memory serves) with John being the active partner. Unfortunately, the other boy had problems with what had happened and told his parents, they in turn complained to the headmaster. The story of what happened got round the school but John's parents refused to move him to another school even though he was being bullied and beaten and was clearly suffering. He mentioned that his parents thought the beatings would change his mind about being gay. It was such a sad story and John was such a lovely boy. He never came back to the group after that first visit and I often wondered what happened to him. I have always thought the main reason why he did not come back was because of a boy (at the group) who tried to pick him up and I have always felt very guilty about not doing more at the time to stop that lad. That lad was already a member of the Teenage Group when I first joined and I found him very predatory. Unfortunately I can't remember his name.[157]

Reflecting on Robert Gibbs' experience and how the group responded, Chris Heaume commented:

The Group dealt well with the issue of predatory greeters. They always found very sound and sensible solutions. The whole atmosphere was so different then, with no spoken professional awareness of abuse, nor training or systems to deal with it. I applied to Centrepoint as an out gay man, to work in their West End team as I knew they had many young gay clients, but they rejected me because it was too risky to appoint an openly gay man, as the Sunday gutter press would take them to the cleaners. The CEO called me in to apologise and explain personally. Such was the atmosphere then, and the context for young people coming out – clandestine and high risk.[158]

The group's first event of the new year was on Sunday 1 January when they went to Bubbles Disco, 19–27 Oxford St., instead of having the usual meeting at Grapevine.

Matthew Bourne started going to the group in March 1978 and continued until February 1979.[159] Matthew Bourne, now Sir Matthew, ballet choreographer, mentioned going along to the group when he was chatting to Jo Whiley on BBC Radio 2 in 2018; he talked about going up the stairs at 296 Holloway Road. He is one of a few former attendees who have become big names. Others include Jimmy Somerville and Andy Bell.

The budget 1977–78 included a fee of £7.50 to affiliate to the London Union of Youth Clubs. An amount of £64.15 was spent on books (this included 20 copies of *Growing up homosexual* at £2 a copy); £75 was spent on adverts in *Gay News*, *Girl about Town* and *Time Out*; and a subscription of three copies was paid for *Gay News*, as well as subscriptions to *Sappho*, *Spare Rib* and *Gay Left*.

In April 1978 the group started a pen pal scheme. The pen pal scheme for under-21s was announced by the LGTG in *Gay News* May 1978.[160] At the group meeting on 9 April members agreed to Toby's (believed to be Toby Keynes) suggestion that the group should become a member of the Gay Activists Alliance. It was also decided that the age limit for new members still had to be enforced at 21. However, the cases of long-serving members who pass 21 would be considered on their individual merits. It was announced that a disco would be held on Sunday 14 May, with Andy and Steve providing the music.[161]

In order to be an established youth group, registration was initially sought with the London Borough of Islington. Registration would bring access to resources and support, as well as validation and security. As Islington Youth Officer Randal Davies explained in May 1978, the process was to be a drawn-out one:

> The group applied to the Area Youth Committee for Islington to become a recognised group. A basic check was made upon the legality of the situation and when no adverse aspects were discovered an application was prepared for Finance and General Purposes Sub Committee who in February [1978] decided to recommend to main committee that the group be recognised. However, before the matter went to main committee County Hall requested that the issue be passed directly to

London Youth Committee for decision by members of Further and Higher Education Committee.

It was decided that the issue should at least be discussed by Area Youth Committee and at their February meeting, after long discussion the committee decided to forward it to L.Y.C. without support and the general concenses [*sic*] seemed one of unwillingness to accept such a registration. From this meeting it was decided to invite Dr Fay Hutchinson to a discussion meeting to talk about Adolescent Sexuality. This proved to be an informative and educational event for most of those attending but notice was taken of the very low attendance.

County Hall took up the matter, first seeking legal advice; the outcome of which reinforced that already gained at local level – that there was no legal reason against accepting the registration.[162]

Filming for a video to support the ILEA application took place at the group on 7 May 1978. Thanks to Steve Power, and then Martin Collins and Chris Heaume, this rare black-and-white footage was kept and uploaded on YouTube in 2013 for private sharing. The title given is: 'London Gay Teenage Group, Black & White Video, shortly before ILEA Registration'.[163] Martin Collins explained how the footage got onto YouTube:

About 25–30 years ago, Steve Power upon leaving the LGTG for pastures new, entrusted a reel of Sony 1" Video tape to my care. I had completely forgotten about it and came across it at my father's house in a box of my stuff stored away. I know that 20 years ago, a college video technician had said it was unplayable. However, with the wonders of modern methods and £100 it has been recovered. A Bristol Company used a baking method to retrieve the recording.[164]

The footage was made to support the application for registration to ILEA and purports to show how the LGTG is a youth club, arranging activities and outings. Individuals are asked about why they attend and also there is some discussion of issues with parents. The surviving recording appears to have been shot on different days at Grapevine. Robert Halls outlines the purpose of the group and points out how the group is mostly made up of young men. The video includes shots of Chris Minter, Robert Gibbs, Steve Power, Steve Lucraft, Andrew Martin, Toby Keynes and others.

Robert Halls was secretary at the LGTG 1977–78 and one of the key people in establishing the group. Robert, born in Edinburgh on 3 October 1958, lived in Carshalton, Surrey, where his parents ran a shop near the railway station. He worked as a librarian. Sadly, like a number of gay men of the time, he died of an AIDS-related illness, aged 34, on 27 February 1993.[165]

In order to get support for the group's registration with ILEA, each Borough Youth Committee was attended. About five or six members of the group would go along and present themselves to the committee and answer any questions committee members might have. Among those who represented the group at these meetings were Steve Power, Robert Halls and Chris Minter.

Opposition to the registration of the LGTG by ILEA came from the London Federation of Boys' Clubs. In a letter their general secretary, AN Gibbs, sent to the principal youth officer at ILEA, DJ McGlynn, their reasons were set out:

> Our experience over many years has taught us that some boys and young men are not sexually orientated until 17 or 18 years of age. It is, therefore, in our view quite wrong to expose boys and young men to the pressures of adult homosexuals who today are increasingly militant and extremely vocal in preaching their particular way of life. We take the view that we cannot employ either in a professional or voluntary capacity any known homosexual, and to the best of our ability we keep a very close watch on the work of anyone who might conceivably have homosexual tendencies... The experience of many leaders in the Boys' Club movement is that those boys in membership who have shown more overt signs of homosexuality during normal adolescent development have, within the healthy atmosphere of a club, grown into normal healthy adjusted young men who have become good husbands and fathers... The Federation readily appreciates that there should be available expert counselling advice, and to make this readily available for the people who most need it it will be necessary to educate our leaders in understanding the particular problems of young homosexuals, and for that matter other deviants who may have problems that at present they cannot discuss with anybody.[166]

Interesting to note that young gay men are called deviants in the letter. Deviant indeed was the view mainstream society had of homosexuality.

Issue 145 of *Gay News* carries a feature on Rose Robertson.[167] Rose remarked that when she started Parents Enquiry in 1968 it was all males but that more recently she had an increasing number of enquiries from lesbians. Once, two girls travelled all the way from Leicester to Catford. 'There was nothing else for them nearer to home. That's what isolation is like'. The feature continued: 'An average day for Rose is a dozen letters and 30 phone calls. Occasionally social services ask her to provide accommodation for young gay people. She also runs a sort of pen pal system where she puts isolated gay youngsters in touch with other isolated youngsters. But this can cause her some worry if it is interpreted as breaking the law (arranging for under-21-year-old males to meet together could be charged as an offence of procuring if they had sex). She works with parents who often feel guilty that their child is gay'.

On 10 June the LGTG had a trip to Oxford. The following day Denis Lemon, editor of *Gay News*, was due to visit the group ('to be confirmed').[168] Lemon had been convicted of blasphemy the previous year for publishing a crude poem about Jesus Christ in *Gay News* in 1976.

In July 1978 the principal youth officer for ILEA prepared a report for the youth committee members on the question of support for youth groups for homosexuals. The report included a summary of the legal advice received: 'the authority itself would not be guilty of a criminal offence merely by the provision or registration of a youth club for homosexuals'.[169] The matter was considered in the light of the law relating to counselling, incitement and conspiracy. If offences were committed on the premises and the authority enabled that, encouraged that, or was reckless as to them occurring, then there would be a serious risk of prosecution. A similar consideration would apply to any officers at the centre. Other organisations in receipt of grants were consulted on an informal basis and 10 of the 15 said they would object to funding of a homosexual youth group. The principal youth officer also consulted the authority's medical advisor. The medical advisor subsequently commented:

I think there is a very real danger that youngsters whose sexual orientation is ambivalent at this stage of their development may well be directed into a homosexual pattern for their adult life by the influence of such a club. It's not for me to say whether a homosexual's life style is sterile and unhappy but it is undoubtedly aberrant.[170]

Comments are then made by the medical advisor about the high rates of sexually transmitted diseases in the homosexual population and that 'half the cases of syphilis in the West End of London are homosexual although they are a small proportion of the sexually active population'.[171]

Support for a teenage gay group did however come from Dr Fay Hutchinson, the medical officer in charge of the London Brook Advisory Centre.[172] Dr Hutchinson was a member of the management committee of the LGTG, and also an advisor to the Islington Area Youth Committee. Chris Heaume recalls that, 'She was a very decent, rounded, professional and supportive person, and wrote a paper to contest that by the ILEA Medical Advisor. It offered some sense and decency and understanding that helped group members a great deal with their arguments'.[173]

The author recalls the wide and diverse range of young people who attended the LGTG:

There was a mix of race, ethnicity, class and lifestyle. Camp, punk, butch, macho, plain, whatever, all attended. While having the common thread of all being regarded as deviant and potentially criminal in the eyes of the law (if we had sex, which quite frankly I think everyone did [but NOT at the group]).

I don't think I knew that it was against the law to have sex with another boy my age... obviously it was against the law to have sex with *children*. But I don't think we were even aware of the fact that the age of consent was 21. I probably became aware of it, at some point. But it didn't even enter my mind?! There were differences but the common bond was strong.[174]

It was refreshing in the late 1970s and early 80s to have a youth group where class, race and ethnicity was not a dividing issue. There were plenty of Black and Asian guys attending the LGTG. In the eyes of mainstream society all were deviant, because they were gay, regardless of the social or racial background they came from. That provided a unity.

In 2018 Claire Lawrie made a film about Black gay people who were in and around London in the 1970s and 80s. In the film, Kenrick Davis mentions going to the gay teenage group in Holloway Road, after ringing them from a telephone box on Portobello Road.[175]

In the summer of 1978 some members of the LGTG attended the Annual Conference of the National Association of Youth Clubs in Sheffield.[176] This was a big moment for the group, being exposed as it were, to straight youths from around the country. Unfortunately, the opportunity to have some of the limelight was hindered by the appearance of Tom O'Carroll of the Paedophile Information Exchange at the Conference. His presence there was controversial. The previous year he had been in the national headlines when PIE held a meeting in London. He was also suspended from his post at the Open University. This was because PIE endorsed sexual relations between adults and children. O'Carroll was allowed to address the NAYC conference but his proposals were voted down. Steve Power recalled the Sheffield NAYC Conference:

> None of us knew that NAYC Exec had invited Tom O'Carroll of PIE to speak at their 1978 annual conference, I believe he was written to by the adult advisers to the committee and was told his invite was to be cancelled, but he had turned up regardless. We didn't even understand who he was at first or what the words PIE stood for. We arrived in the big hall at the Uni and the atmosphere was electrifying. It was buzzing with confusion, controversy and huge activity. An announcement was made on stage that the executive had accepted an offer of a talk by Tom O' Carroll of PIE, but given recent events they were as a committee being advised not to go ahead. We were asked as members (the whole audience) if they should allow him to speak, as they had been advised not to. The national press, university officials and advisers to NAYC were there. It was explained what Mr O'Carroll was to talk about. I soon realised that this was the man who had been in the *Sunday Mirror* the previous year for holding a meeting at Conway Hall in London, I kind of recalled the news headlines of people who had been beaten, kicked and punched. The paper had named various folk attending and I recalled the blood on folks' faces who had been beaten up. The paper was outraged they were meeting. So I soon realised this was a continuation of this saga and their attempt to get recognised. This may seem strange but my immediate thoughts were: "Jeez our attendance was upstaged by this damn controversial bloke, I just wish he would piss off!'[177]

After the press stuff about PIE [Paedophile Information Exchange], Andrew [Martin], I believe, attended a meeting most likely at London Friend that was discussing them, he wanted to suss it out. He reported back that PIE would know of us but they had enough sense not to approach us! Andrew was a formidable punk and frightened most folk.[178]

Andrew Martin and Alan Williams produced a magazine called *Metro* which featured a lot of LGTG news. Edition no 8 of 5 November 1978 has a piece by Robert Halls on the front page. He mentions a new person attending the group two weeks previously and that only two members spoke to him briefly. 'Why was this?' he asks. 'He wasn't physically repellent, he didn't smell or look aggressive – maybe it was because the group is now one large clique… It is pointless looking for culprits – you are all to blame – but the danger is that if this continues, the group will very rapidly vanish up its own arse.'

Homosexuality was still a taboo subject in schools in 1978. Dr Paulina Palmer pointed this out in a letter to *The Guardian* in which she cogently outlined the problems gay teenagers faced:

The homosexual youngster grows up surrounded by a miasma of silence and misinformation. While aware that she is out of step with her peers, she may as yet be unable to define her sexual preferences and, since she has no models to enlighten her, may retreat from human contact into a state of introverted depression.

Dr Palmer went on to state the 'especially distressful position of the male homosexual teenager for whom the legal age of consent stands at the ludicrously high figure of 21'.[179] The author seems to recall reading this letter at the time and finding it very encouraging that someone who would be taken seriously (an academic in Cambridge) understood his position.

A Conference on Young Gays was held at Grapevine in Holloway Road on 7 October 1978, and a follow-up meeting held on Saturday 25 November at the same venue. Organisations represented at the first conference were CHE, Parents Enquiry, Icebreakers, Gay Switchboard, Grapevine, Leicester Gayline & Teenage Group, London Gay Teenage Group, North Westminster Detached Youth Project, London Friend and Lesbian Line.

Notes of the initial meeting state: 'This conference of a number of representatives of voluntary organisations providing helping services to gay teenagers was convened by Micky Burbidge (Icebreakers). Its purpose was to consider what action should be taken in consequence of the Home Secretary's recent undertaking to Mary Whitehouse that he would "investigate" organisations concerned to help young gay people'. The meeting recognised the demand for services noted by Switchboard and other telephone helplines. It also noted that there were three gay teenage groups in existence and that more were needed 'because gay teenagers want to meet each other and because the "pub and club scene" is often sordid and predatory'. A provisional title for a group was 'Gay

Teenage Support Group'. Two working parties were set up to explore specific proposals to be considered at the next meeting and to collate information on the number of calls organisations receive from young gays.[180] It was at the second meeting that the title of the Joint Council for Gay Teenagers was adopted. It was also agreed to invite the following organisations: Samaritans, Release, NUS, NUSS and Capital Helpline. Administration was provided by Micky Burbidge, who lived at 26 Dresden Road, N19. His day job was in the civil service and he had been involved in the Counter-Psychiatry Group.[181] The Joint Council for Gay Teenagers formed out of these meetings. JCGT aimed to encourage such initiatives as the LGTG nationally, through publicity and through helping groups to make connections with each other. At the meeting of the JCGT in January 1979 the organisations represented included Bristol Gay Switchboard, Earl's Court Gay Helpline, London Friend, Friend Merseyside and National Friend, Befriending Group, Icebreakers, West Midlands Gay Switchboard, LGTG, Leicester Gayline & Teenage Group, Merseyside Gay Youth Group, and Parents Enquiry. Publicity aimed at the youth work and gay press was provided through press releases on the rationale and methodologies for gay youth work, supported by a series of leaflets and two booklets, *I know what I am* (1980) and *Breaking the Silence* (1981) (edited by Michael Burbidge and Jonathan Walters).

JCGT enabled groups to link through a series of events including two youth camps in the Peak District, and weekend visits between London and Liverpool groups. Helping Michael (Micky) Burbidge to set up the JCGT were two youth workers who were members or attenders of the management committee of the London Gay Teenage Group – Jonathan Walters and Chris Heaume. The JCGT submitted a response to the Home Office Policy Advisory Committee on the age of consent and organised a delegation to Parliament to lobby for a reduction in the age for homosexual activity to 16.

The JCGT helped to establish the Gay Youth Movement (GYM) which was set up in 1980. Following the development of the GYM, the JCGT disbanded, its mission having been achieved. Formal closure was approved at a meeting on 30 August 1982 when the management committee agreed 'over the next year' that the JCGT 'will be wound down and all its areas of work absorbed by the Gay Youth Movement'.[182]

CHE Executive Meeting Minutes 16 December 1978 approve support for the JCGT and £5 towards the JCGT.[183] At the time CHE were promoting a Tape/Slide Education Kit. The kit was banned from use in Tyneside, where Tyneside CHE had originally produced the package, but the ban had the effect of generating more interest in it. Bishopsgate Institute have a copy of the kit.[184]

The tape/slide project started in 1972 and took a long time to become complete. It was still not ready in February 1976.[185]

In autumn 1978 the LGTG were looking for new premises. There was a possible new venue in Park Square, near Great Portland Street, owned by an organisation called Play Space for Children.[186] An appeal was printed in *Gay News*. Premises required to be spacious with canteen facilities and room for a pool table and record player.[187] At the end of the year Robert Halls resigned as secretary and John Stevens agreed to take on the role. Activities organised by members of the group included a trip to the Rocky Horror Show organised by Steve Lucraft. An 'Outside Activities Group' was formed to 'get people of [sic] their behinds and into some form of sport or games, although this has now been extended to punk gigs'.[188]

Rock singer Tom Robinson wrote to Steve Power (8 November 1978) saying that he hoped to visit the group on Sunday 3 December. He would bring an acoustic guitar. Following the visit which took place as planned, a group of members went to McDonald's in Seven Sisters Road. This was a regular after-group rendezvous, with its milkshakes and French fries. On this particular Sunday something happened which annoyed Andrew Martin and he typed up a page lambasting certain people:

> The bigoted behaviour in McDonald's afterwards annoyed me enough to get out this typewriter once again. These people who know who I mean. I apologise to all those who this doesn't apply to.
>
> …They're jealous of our ability to be open, frank, truthful and genuine about ourselves and our problems and our lifestyles. It is not our fault they don't understand us. It's all their hang up, not ours. If they get aggravated by this, like, these trendy middle class bigots who can't understand people like me, well sorry, sweetie, but while you were worried about the state of Mummy's Axminster carpet, we were being kicked around by our dads and clocking our lives away in a factory. How many of you lot, with your public school university and cars and your plastic anger with RAR [Rock Against Racism] badges, how many of you have ever been beaten up inside a police station? You think it's funny to take the piss out of people like me… I don't sing you're glad to be gay, because I'm not.[189]

The diatribe went on and on and clearly Andrew was upset. He remained an enigma at the group, but he certainly worked hard at keeping it going.

In February 2020 the author met Tom Robinson at an event at the Bishopsgate Institute in London and took the opportunity to thank him for coming to the group in 1978! He recalled going into McDonald's after he visited us and then finding some of the group coming in and one or two remarks about him being in there! Maybe it was the camp members saying something like 'Fancy meeting a pop star in McDonald's', or something like that. I wonder if this is what upset Andrew Martin. It certainly left an impression on Tom Robinson to mention it over 41 years later!

Tom Robinson's record had Gay Switchboard's telephone number on the sleeve. This was an important source of information which enabled many to discover gay venues and organisations, including the LGTG.

In an interview with researcher Martha Rhodes Robinson, the author recalled the visit of Tom Robinson:

> We had some key people come to see us. Tom Robinson, who was in the charts, you know, 'Glad to Be Gay'.[190] So it was great fun... we met Tom Robinson! And we knew who he was because we'd heard his record and seen him on *Top of the Pops*. And he came and saw us, played his guitar and signed autographs for us. And then we had another rock star, called Wayne County or Jane County of Wayne County and the Electric Chairs, that was her band. And my mate, who was very keen on the band, he was very excited when she came along. And after she left the group we got on the bus together with her, and went off – went off to have a drink with her. There was also a radio programme on Radio London broadcast by a man called Malcolm Laycock, he did a talk show. I remember I either wrote to him, or I phoned him up, and he was, you know, pleased to have some gay young people talking to him on the radio. Which was quite revolutionary in 1978–79.[191]

Michael Connew recalled a couple of other visitors to the LGTG:

> I have happy memories of some of the visitors we had at Holloway Road. I remember Bryan Derbyshire (Beryl to his friends) paid a visit. He was a publisher and journalist and went on to run Mr Gay UK. He gave us a wonderful chat about his life and how he had come out, very amusing as I recall. The other visit I remember was from a young actor by the name of Nigel Townsend. He gave a workshop

on improvisation and relaxation. He went on to manage the YMCA youth touring company 'Y Touring'. We still occasionally run into each other.[192]

A Christmas party was held on Sunday 24 December 1978 at Grapevine.

Chapter Six

MANOR GARDENS, LONDON, N7. LONDON GAY TEENAGE GROUP REGISTERS AS A YOUTH GROUP.

The Observer magazine in January 1979 included a small feature about gay teenagers. The article mentioned the work of Parents Enquiry. Colin Sinclair was featured wearing a tartan shirt and dungarees. Colin said, 'It would be good for other kids to feel that homosexuality was a subject that could be talked about quite openly and freely'. Telephone numbers were listed for Icebreakers, Parents Enquiry and Lesbian Line.[193]

The notes of a LGTG meeting held 2 February 1979, with convenor Simon Gregor, mentions selling Gay Pride '79 badges at the group as a means of fundraising for the LGTG. It is reported that the group funds stand at approximately £100.

The real threat that those organising the group might be prosecuted for conspiracy to corrupt public morals was discussed at length in the notes of the same meeting.

Under the heading 'Prosecution':

At the moment there is no concern for alarm. We have heard from two legal sources about a case which refers to conspiring, counselling or incitement to commit an illegal act. Rumours suggest it will be a north London gay group. So it is something we must be wary and conscious of. E.g. people who approach the group, answering telephone calls etc.[194]

It is also reported that: 'Grapevine are moving at the end of March to premises near the Angel underground station. If the LGTG go there also they would be sharing premises with the Islington Girls Project. With office space and phone bills about £1,000 would be needed' (presumably per annum). The LGTG were also looking at other premises. The meeting notes Jane Dixon has been asked to come to the group to help the girls within the group. The CHE Monday Group had donated £50 after the talk Neville and Philip gave them.[195]

A letter from Micky Burbidge to Steve Power outlines that Rose Robertson had found out that Mary Whitehouse had had two meetings with Margaret Thatcher (then Leader of the Opposition in the House of Commons). The letter says 'MW and "her cronies" are setting up a group to investigate groups for young gay people. It is what we must expect… It is Rose's opinion that if the Tories come to power (which could be in April) Mrs Thatcher would set up an official investigation of some kind'.[196]

In February 1979 the *Daily Telegraph* reported that the National Association of Boys' Clubs (NABC) vigorously opposed the application to register homosexual clubs within the Inner London Education Authority Youth Service. The association wrote to ILEA urging it not to set a dangerous precedent and pointing out that many youngsters were not sexually orientated until they were 17 or 18, and that exposing them to the 'hot house of a purely sexually orientated environment' was unfair.[197] In order to achieve recognition by ILEA as a youth club, the LGTG issue was debated by all the separate youth committees in each of the ILEA boroughs. Members of the group visited each of the authorities and addressed the youth committees.

A collective meeting on 2 March was chaired by Chris Heaume. There was discussion of trying to organise a benefit gig. The funds stood at approximately £80. Neville, who was not present at the meeting, wanted to give up the post of treasurer and Dave was willing to take on the role. A trip to Lemons Disco was being arranged by Nick Dobie (March 23 meet 9pm outside Grapevine – £1.50 each). Chris Minter was setting up a photographic group. It was reported that 10 of the 12 ILEA Youth Area Committees were supporting the group's application for registration. One group was still to be visited (Lambeth). One group was opposed (not named). Grapevine had been given an extension on the premises until July. It was reported that the new Grapevine premises (they moved to 416 St John St, EC1) would be too small, but the possibility of premises at the North London Welfare Centre (Manor Gardens) was looking good. The new caretaker at Manor Gardens was sympathetic and would be raising the possibility at their committee meeting on 4 April. Max was arranging a speaker from Grapevine to talk to the group about VD. Phil was getting a new needle for the record player.

Numbers attending the group had dropped off a bit recently. 'A point was raised concerning the exhibitionism shown by various members. The group is a place where people can be themselves, it would be wrong of us to ask them to change. All that we can ask is that members behave reasonably on and outside the Grapevine premises'.[198]

This latter point is one that would feature as a theme throughout the life of the group. The more extrovert and particularly 'camp' members could appear overwhelming, particularly for new and often very shy members. One person remarked in *Breaking the Silence* that he went to the LGTG and found that they were 'a bunch of poofters so stopped going'.[199]

Under the heading 'Age': 'After the unfortunate occurrences of last month, many people were driven away some unnecessarily. It is not desirable that the group be dominated by older people, but cases should be decided upon taking the individual into consideration'. Subsequent ILEA registration required that the age bracket 16 minimum age and 21 maximum age be adhered to.

The meeting notes that a discussion group would start up on Wednesday (at the Kentish Town Detached Youth Work Project, Caversham Road). The first one to be run by Icebreakers. John Stevens announced that he would be stepping down as secretary. Steve and Andy were taking over as secretary on a temporary basis. The group would need a new chair soon as 'Steve fades out'. Steve Power remained chair until June 1980. The LGTG decided not to affiliate with Rose Robertson's Parents Enquiry 'as this may jeopardise her position'. It was noted that three members of the Manchester Gay Teenage Group would visit the LGTG soon.

The Christian morality Festival of Light campaign newsletter *Nationwide Bulletin* no 5 referred to the LGTG's application to register as a youth club. The bulletin says these young people should be welcomed into mainstream youth clubs and offered help there 'so that they might become normal members of society … The medical and moral implications of a youth club catering specifically for homosexuals, on the other hand, are very serious indeed'. The bulletin goes on to describe such a group as 'morally corrupting'.[200]

From 16–22 April 12 members of the group went on a camping trip to Marchant's Hill Campsite, Surrey.[201] Evening visits were made to Bunters, Guildford and a party in Farnham (private house).[202] The group also went horse riding and to the beach at West Wittering. The trip cost each participant £8.50. The author recalls that when in Chichester the group saw the Conservative candidate Anthony Nelson (the 1979 General Election campaign was on at the time) and challenged him about gay law reform. He replied that he had met with the Campaign for Homosexual Equality to discuss homosexual issues. Of the three main political parties, only the Liberal Party mentioned 'gay rights' in their manifesto.[203]

The aims and objectives of the LGTG were drawn up in April 1979:

The London Gay Teenage Group aims to offer young homosexuals support and friendship in an environment conducive to personal growth, unrestricted by the pressures and limitations that are encountered elsewhere.

The object is to offer a group situation where young homosexuals can:

i.   relax.
ii. make friends of their own age.
iii. become more aware of their own sexuality, whether it be homosexual, heterosexual or bisexual.
iv. support each other in gaining confidence and in being better prepared for the pressures that can be encountered at home, at school, at work and elsewhere.
v.   find an alternative to the anonymity and isolation of the commercial gay scene.
vi. seek counselling and advice on specific problems, such as those to do with work, accommodation or personal difficulties.
vii. enjoy themselves.[204]

The LGTG committee elected on 20 May 1979 was: Maureen Hand, Zoe Pitt, Andrew Leo Martin, Alf Florence, Helen Tucker, Shelia, Peter Langford. Twelve people put their names forward. The next election was to be Sunday 18 November (six months' service).[205]

Steve Power dealt with pen pals and put correspondents who lived a long way from London in touch with others.

The group were seeking new premises having had to vacate 296 Holloway Road after they had had a fire on the premises (in the part of the building occupied below by a takeaway). Manor Gardens Centre, 6–9 Manor Gardens, N7 6LA (North Islington Welfare Centre) was approached and offered to hire out a hall for £5 a session plus 60p per session for the office/telephone access (subject to the agreement of their committee).[206] In May 1979 Manor Gardens committee said yes to the LGTG subject to ILEA approval (although the committee would also consider the LGTG if ILEA did not approve the application).[207]

In June 1979 a leaflet produced by Andrew Martin stated that, thanks to Val Marshall, the group received a grant from the London Union of Youth Clubs, to whom the group had been affiliated for two years. The group were still waiting for the outcome of their application to ILEA to register as a youth club. There was no chairman/person listed for the group, but the following positions are listed:

Organiser/secretary: Andrew Martin
Co-ordinator: Maureen Hand
Treasurer: Tony Baker
PR and guest speakers: Zoe Pitt[208]

In 2020 Steve Power recalled one of the meetings LGTG members attended in the process of seeking to be accepted as an official youth group:

We had to turn up and do a presentation at County Hall to the London Youth Committee. The only youth group in its history to be asked to justify itself. We showed a film and answered questions and we had to listen to groups who were for and anti our registration. The London Scouts were there and tried to block our registration. I was pretty nervous that evening as I am sure others were, the atmosphere was formal and tense. We were adamant that we wanted to put our case across and not let this Committee off the hook in terms of its obligations. One of the groups who were anti our registration The Scouts made a statement on the night. They stated they had undertaken research that established that young gay folk were causing physical harm to themselves as well as emotional harm, and this would lead to medical issues in later life. They stated they had evidence that homosexuality caused a weakening of the anal sphincter.[209] In questioning them as part of the debate I asked them how they had conducted this research and stated that I could only assume through their membership? The place fell about in laughter. The funny thing is how things come full circle. I am now about to be appointed as the chairperson of a district scout group where I live and they know I am gay and they accept it without issue. Amazing really what we achieved.[210]

On 22 June 1979 the principal youth officer at ILEA wrote to Steve Power of the LGTG informing him that ILEA would now accept official registration of the group with their local Area Youth Committee. This had been agreed at the meeting of the London Youth Committee on 11 June 1979, although the decision needed to be ratified by the Further and Higher Education Committee. This was reported in *Gay News* at the end of June.[211]

As Chris Heaume recalled in January 2019:

A formal management committee was required when we got our ILEA registration, were funded to appoint a worker that the ILEA employed and seconded to us, and when we received the grant for the research project… I left around that point as Gregg [Blachford] was in post.[212]

Woman's Hour on BBC Radio 4 featured: 'Talking Point: what are the problems of teenage homosexuals and how can they and their parents cope with them? Reading Your Letters'. Rose Robertson and John Sketchley were on the programme that was broadcast live on Thursday 28 June. This followed an interview with three teenage gays broadcast 25 June: 'Coming Out in Your Teens: three teenagers talk about being homosexual'.[213]

In the summer of 1979 the teenage group was part of the Gay Pride week committee. 'Three People' were three teenagers (Rikki Beadle, Robert Chevara and Michelle Baugham), who provided entertainment at one of the events held at Oval House, 52 Kennington Oval, SE 11.

The Young Lesbian group was set up in mid-1979 by workers at the Islington Girls Project, meeting on Monday nights. The number of lesbians attending the main LGTG had always been low and many of those who attended did not return. By having a separate group for lesbians it was hoped that newcomers would be more likely to return and this proved the case. Some lesbians continued to attend the main LGTG but the numbers attending the YLG was much greater.

At the beginning of September the group was in new premises, having done the cleaning and decorating themselves – work and commitment which impressed the Manor Gardens Centre committee. Subsequent stories that the hall used by the group once had a mortuary table in it have proved, to date, to be a myth. The hall had previously been the laundry for the Manor Gardens Centre. A phone was installed when the LGTG moved in.

Overseeing and supporting the LGTG (from 1979) was a management committee, mostly adults with access to resources and support. Chris Heaume, in a letter sent with the agenda for the first management committee held at Manor Gardens on 4 September, outlined the way the group was run:

> ... in September it is hoped that the group will become a registered ILEA youth group, after two years of educating within ILEA. This will mean more secure funding and the support and backing of a large and important youth service. To consolidate all of this we will be looking to the Management Committee for their support and practical help. The people we have asked to be on the committee share a variety of skills, including youth work skills, knowledge of how to use youth service resources, counselling skills and a positive awareness of homosexuality and the gay scene. By sharing all this with the Group and its members, we hope that the committee will help the Group to continue to thrive and develop, to overcome difficulties as they arise, and to offer a sound service to young gay people in London.
>
> As some members of the Group will also be involved on the Management Committee, some help and support will be able to be offered at meetings. But we hope too that various members of the committee will be able to take an active interest in the actual work of the Group by spending time with Group members at the three weekly sessions, and also away from the Group. The Group has always been one that looks after itself, motivates itself, and does its own work – member involvement is probably its most important aspect – and a large part of the role of the Management Committee will be to help stimulate, train and support members in their own involvement in running and working with the Group. Whilst Jane Dixon and I, who both play these roles at the moment, will continue to support and service the Group as long as it needs it, hopefully we will come to a time where the Group is self-sufficient![214]

The members of the management committee on 4 September were: Steve Power (LGTG chairman), Andrew Martin (secretary), Alan Williams (treasurer), Maureen Hand (group representative), Brian Earl (Manor Gardens), Patrick Hacker (social worker), Gerard Hendra (London Friend), Fay Hutchinson (Brook Advisory Service), Winston Pinder (youth officer, Islington), Rose Robertson (Parents Enquiry) and Brian Travers (detached youth worker, Westminster). All except Rose Robertson were able to attend the meeting at Manor Gardens on 4 September. Also attending were Chris Heaume, Gary Barker, Jaime Rogers, Alan Makepiece, Thomas Flanagan and Keith Andrews. Membership of the committee changed from time to time.

The first actual group meeting at the Manor Gardens Centre was on 9 September. The hall where the group met is now called the Dame Geraldine Hall and in 2018 was housing the Autism Partnership[215]. The magazine produced by Andrew Martin noted that 58 people turned up for the first meeting of the group at Manor Gardens and that nine of those people were new.[216]

This new home gave the growing group a small hall, small meeting room and an office, with lawns outside. An ILEA youth officer found the group a pool table, a table tennis table and such like. There was space for the group to breathe, to be active, to mix, chat and have fun, and to run its own affairs. Rooms in the main building were sometimes used for projects.

At this time LGTG had a group committee organised by Andrew Martin and Maureen Hand. This committee, made up of young members, coordinated the activities and day-to-day running of the group. At a meeting of the management committee on 26 September 1979 the possibility of employing a paid youth worker was discussed. Applications were made in 1980 and 1981, eventually leading to success and an appointment in 1982.[217]

On 26 September 1979 Islington Area Youth Office wrote to Andrew Martin to inform him that the ILEA Youth Committee for Islington approved the application for registration of the London Gay Teenage Group at their meeting on 24 September 1979. Not only did this provide recognition which could shield the group from more negative forces, it also provided access to expertise, advice, resources and support. A youth officer was assigned to help link the group to such things and to help with applications for financial support for rent and running costs, equipment, project funding and workers. This recognition from the largest statutory UK youth service provided important encouragement to other gay youth groups around the country.

In a leaflet produced by the group around this time, Chris Heaume is mentioned as a detached youth worker and Steve Power as assisting with outside contacts.[218]

A television drama series called *Kids* was broadcast on LWT (London Weekend Television). The episode shown at 9pm on Friday 25 May was called 'Michael and Liam', and featured a 15-year-old gay boy (Liam) who had been caught soliciting, for which he was placed in a children's home (Kingston House). There another boy (Michael) suffering severe depression joined him, after making a suicide attempt. Their relationship was explored in what, for the time, was a ground-breaking drama. Liam was played by Jason Kemp and Michael by Paul Easom. The director was John Frankau. Such a depiction of gay teenagers was rare on British television at the time. The *Daily Mirror* TV guide called it a 'Gay Play Puzzler', and went on to describe how 15-year-old Liam being sent to a children's home was like letting 'a rabbit patrol a lettuce patch'. The *Mirror* then asks: 'The big question is: does the homosexual corrupt the normal straight youth or might the bent bewildered lad get straightened out?'[219]

The Albany Trust's report 'Youth and Sexuality' produced at this time and reporting on their Department of Education-sponsored project, was over 50 pages long.[220]

Martin Collins recalls growing up as a gay teenager and first attending the group in 1979:

I can remember hearing at the Kenneth More Theatre that there were Helplines and once or twice during my teens, probably at 15–16, recall scanning through the phone books and yellow pages looking under all the slang terms I had been called at school, looking for something, but without knowing the term GAY or Homosexual, I found nothing.

I saw plenty of messages on the walls of toilets at Piccadilly Circus tube, Stratford Station and other stations closer to my home station at Woodford on the Central Line. I hung around these toilets a lot, but until I was 18 nothing ever happened as I was too scared and I think the men I saw were scared of me too.

Lisa [best friend at Loughton F.E. College] told me that Glen [Glen Perry, East 15 Acting School] went to a gay youth club in Holloway and I might like to go along. Glen told me the address. I drove my dad's car there a few times, parked outside watching young people going in and coming out, locking the gate, and each time I wanted to go in but was too nervous.

Then one Sunday, whilst sitting watching, trying to pluck up the courage to go in, along minced Glen Perry. I was out of the car in a shot because here was someone I knew. I followed him in, I don't remember much about that very first entrance, but do dearly remember a punk guy offering me a coffee – Andy Martin. There was a collection made that session but I was excused as it was my first session. However I soon realised this was one of the few ways the group raised money.

This first visit was probably mid-1979 as I was going there whilst my mother was in her last year on this earth. I know I must have become a regular. I can remember that when I started attending, Steve Power either had just stood down as chair or was in the throes of doing so and Gary Barker became chairman...

After most group sessions on a Sunday afternoon, a lot of members would go to the Wimpy burger bar, known as the Buggery Bar, for a snack and then either the Euston Tavern or The Black Cap. When I had use of dad's car I was a taxi service, but often didn't feel I could stay very long as I didn't want to raise awkward questions at home.

In some ways using dad's car rather than public transport rather isolated me from group activities.

I do not recall how many sessions I'd been to, it seems in my memory to have been very few. One Sunday, I think it was, there was a committee meeting and Chris Heaume announced that 'Martin has agreed to become our treasurer' or words to that effect. Even then I was pedantic about facts, and I very distinctly remember turning to Chris and saying 'No, I said I'd have a go!' And that was the start of my involvement. I remember the previous treasurer looking somewhat relieved.

I initially continued with Barclays but because I knew of some associations with South Africa and thus the apartheid regime, I opened a new bank account with NatWest Bank and closed the Barclays one. I expect this was agreed with Chris Heaume &/or Gary Barker, but I think it was my idea. Looking at the fact that we owed over a year's rent to MGC [Manor Gardens Centre] and I don't think we'd actually claimed much grant aid from ILEA which was primarily 50% of our premises rent costs, together with the fact that there wasn't much in the bank account, some serious fundraising was required. This is the term I now know, back then it was just how can we raise money.[221]

In October *Gay News* ran an article on setting up gay youth groups. It described the work of the JCGT. The article covers issues about recruitment, induction, age, leadership, finance, structure of the group, composition of the group and relationships with other groups. 'There is evidence in JCGT's survey and elsewhere that lesbians tend to come out later than gay men. So there are fewer gay teenage women about. Woman are almost bound to be a minority in a gay teenage group', reports *Gay News*. At the time the article was published there were still very few gay teenage groups and no lesbian teenage group.[222] Micky Burbidge, who helped to establish the JCGT, surveyed the gay switchboards and other helplines around the country requesting data on how many calls they took from young people. Forty-one questionnaire forms were returned and an analysis done estimating the number of calls under-21 people may have made to such help organisations each year. Burbidge concluded that 'it seems likely that some 12,000 teenagers a year are currently seeking help or advice from gay organisations in the United Kingdom. In the case of all male teenagers aged 14 to 20 in England and Wales this represents about one in every 300. In the case of female teenagers, it is fewer than 1 in every 1,000'.[223] The estimates were more precisely reported when the results of the survey were published in *I know what I am* (1980).

CHE had a representative on the JCGT. Andy Armitage was minuted to attend.[224] Generally, there is however almost nothing about under-21s or gay teenagers in CHE executive committee minutes for 1979, save a minute of the meeting on April 21 which states: 'CHE now has observer membership of the British Youth Council'.

The *Daily Telegraph* reported in November 1979 about the Royal Court Theatre's 'Young People's Theatre Project' organising a Youth and Sexuality forum. Rose Robertson of Parents Enquiry was among those involved. The *Telegraph* questioned who was funding this where the 'general purpose [is] to do what it can in its little way to help confuse and subvert our society'.[225] This prompted a letter from Antony Grey to Bill Deedes, editor of the newspaper.[226]

Thomas Flanagan recalled:

I was class of 79, a young 17-year-old Irish boy who fled the troubles in Northern Ireland to find himself and did so in the LGTG: my life today and happiness started there and for that I will be eternally grateful … Keith Andrews my first ever boyfriend, who sadly died in 1994, who I met at the LGTG in 1979 and who became (as far as I'm aware) the first openly gay elected member on the National Association of Youth Clubs [NAYC] executive committee after the LGTG went to the annual conference in 1979, which I believe was held in Leeds that year. I also remember going to a conference in Hull/Grimsby the following year but could have been the other way round, either way it was a great achievement for the LGTG at the time.[227]

In December 1979 the Joint Council for Gay Teenagers (JCGT) met in Liverpool at the Link Centre, 14 Colquitt Street. Steve Power reported that he had details of 13 gay youth groups in Britain. Tony Salvas reported that some gay counselling services had adopted a minimum age for counsellors at 21. JCGT agreed that its disapproval of this practice be minuted.[228] In the evening those who had been at the meeting went to a gay bar in Stanley Street, Liverpool. One member ended up in the Bridewell just off Dale Street.[229] Just before Christmas 10 members of the LGTG went on a day trip to Boulogne.[230]

Chapter Seven

GAY YOUTH MOVEMENT LAUNCHED, 1980

In January 1980 the 'Young gay women (up to 21) group' (London) were listed under that description in *Gay News*.[231] This was still a time when the term gay could refer to men or women. As the decade evolved the gay women tended to use the term lesbian in preference to gay.

In March 1980 Geoffrey Brighton, a 20-year-old student at Leeds University, was refused a medical certificate of fitness to teach by the Student Health Service because of his homosexuality.[232] London Weekend Television broadcast 11 episodes of *Gay Life* in 1980 (first series) and 1981 (second series). In 1981 an episode titled 'Male Sexuality' featured Greg Hayman, then aged 22, and his former partner Simon Watney, age 32, art lecturer. Greg had previously attended the LGTG. He was active in the Labour Party[233] and later became Mayor of Cromer in 2011.

The LGTG appeared in *Mister*, a gay soft porn magazine (vol 3 no 2). The group had decided it was good publicity if any youngsters learned about the group through seeing the article. Those members happy to appear included Neville Magee, Royce Ullah, Chris Minter, Keith Ramathal, Roy Puddefoot, Chris Cleary and Jimmy Somerville (who later became a well-known pop star). Jim (Jimmy), age 18, stated he had: 'started cottaging at 15 and slipping into gay pubs.' *Mister* further reports that 'George goes to the Hemingford Arms on Friday nights. That's Icebreakers disco and he likes it because it is friendly. A boon at the GTG [*sic*] meetings is the non-cruisy atmosphere enjoyed by the teenagers. Although they often subsequently go out with each other, there are no sexual encounters at the group and no trace of the pressure found on the open gay scene.'[234]

Icebreakers ran the disco at the Hemingford Arms, Offord Road, Islington. It started there in the summer of 1979 after they moved their disco from the

Prince Albert, near King's Cross Station (the Prince Albert is now called Central Station)[235]. A visit to the Icebreakers disco was recorded by 'Gaywaves' radio in 1982.[236] In 1983 The Bell at King's Cross became the venue for the disco.[237]

At the end of May a group of LGTG attenders went to West Mersea in Essex to join a youth camp event. Kevin O'Neill recalls:

It was the late May bank holiday of 1980 to an ILEA funded/run campsite in Essex. On the second night we went to a club or bar in the local town (Colchester or Chelmsford, I'm not sure). The entrance was via a pedestrian subway at a major traffic junction. The door was metal with an eye level, letterbox size hatch, very high security. Our responsible adult, which I think must have been Chris Heaume, knocked, explained to the bouncer that yes, we knew it was a gay venue and yes, we were all gay. He also obscured the bouncer's view so he couldn't see how young we all were, some underage no doubt. We got in, it was very quiet and rather disappointing. I'm sure it was a Sunday evening, so not surprising really.[238]

In 1980 the author attended a conference for German/British youth in the Hartz Mountains area of Germany at Sonnenberg:

It was Chris Heaume who arranged for me to go to an event in Germany – in the Hartz Mountains. We had group discussions on minorities (all translated from German to English and vice versa). One of the opening questions was 'Is there a particular minority that you identify with?' Some lads from the East End who had travelled over on the boat with me said: 'We're Bengali and we live in London, you know, we're a minority group but there's quite a lot of us in East London' or whatever. And then it came to me and I said, 'Well, I'm gay', and it was like 'woah, blimey!' I remember everyone seemed surprised when I told them I was gay. It was unusual for a young person to say that, then.

I had gone on my own but was confident. The interpreter, working on German-English translations at the conference, came up to me afterwards and congratulated me for being so bold and bought me a snaps.

The following year, in June 1981, 10 members of the LGTG, along with Chris Heaume and Jonathan Walters, attended a similar conference on minorities at Sonnenberg.

July 1980 saw several members attend the NAYC conference in Hull where the weekend was titled 'Where's the sense? But what the hell!' Attenders from the ILEA area were able to get a small grant towards the cost of attending.[239]

On 23 June 1980 Steve Power stepped down as chair of the group. Steve pointed out that each group session cost the group £17.25 on average and fundraising was needed to avoid being in debt. Use of the pool table raised about £20 each month. An item about youth workers and the group noted that the youth workers' help was all voluntary and they were under a lot of work pressure. A rota was suggested. This was thought to be a good idea in the same way that women youth workers supported the Young Lesbian nights. A new committee would be elected on 8 September.[240] Islington Area Youth Office supported the group with grants and from 1982 part-time youth worker hours.[241] ILEA paid grants of 25% of the costs of rent, increased to 50% from April 1981.

Martin Collins (treasurer) explained how the costs and ILEA grant was managed:

Manor Gardens (Brian Earl centre coordinator) would supply handwritten invoices to the LGTG for rent which included electric & water usage, itemising the dates that month that we used the premises. We would then technically have paid MGC [Manor Gardens Centre] and had the invoices annotated as received. I would then every few months (6 monthly I think), submit these to ILEA County Hall SE1 and receive a cheque payable to the LGTG for 50% of the rent invoices.

However, as the LGTG was always so broke, I would pay the MGC 50% of rent or whatever we could afford and Brian Earl would supply invoices saying we had paid, for me to submit to the ILEA, and then when we received the cheque, pay the rest and give me a receipt slip. It was quite complicated juggling what was paid and what was not. But Brian and I from time to time, would sit down and work out where we were at.

It was complicated by the fact that there was a period between ILEA Registration (I don't know the date) and me coming into office, where none of rent was claimed and the invoices went missing. So initially I was playing catch up and had to plead that the rent grant be honoured for a previous financial year. I think (maybe) that the LGTG did not fully understand that receipted invoices had to be submitted to

County Hall. I think it was assumed that magically the ILEA would pay MGC with no paperwork. The world doesn't work like that. [242]

I know what I am: gay teenagers and the law was published by the JCGT in 1980. This was a joint effort. Credit was given to me (the author of this book) for helping with the organisation and analysis of the survey (see introduction by Robert Longley). The booklet contains several quotes from gay teenagers reflecting the isolation, prejudice and ignorance they faced. Here are two such cases from the book:

I was depressed about covering it up… saying I like pictures of girls… telling lies… you have to do it. I was depressed about not being able to talk to someone about it. When my sister says 'When are you going to get a girlfriend?' then I feel God I wish I was straight. When I am with David I feel safe, safer than when I am at home. At home I have to call people queers. [Adam, 16, Ipswich].

Two years ago I painfully realised that for the rest of my life I would be homosexual, there was no more 'maybe I'll change as I get older'. I became dreadfully unhappy, crying almost every night. Now I am adjusting and things are not so bad, but I still need someone's help. [Glen, 18, Harlow].

The booklet also reported on the survey, conducted by the JCGT, of all gay help services in the UK covering a two-week period in February 1979. This collated information on how many teenagers were contacting the services and what sort of issues were being dealt with. Based on that sample it was estimated that anything between 6,370 and 16,754 young people aged 14–20 contacted gay help services in one year. Twenty-five per cent of those calls were from 14–16-year-olds. Males made up 85% of the teenage callers.

Following the publication of *I know what I am*, a delegation of the JCGT made a lobby presentation to MPs in the House of Commons on 7 July. Six MPs attended (Joe Ashton, Labour; Charles Irving, Conservative; Ian Mikado, Labour; Allan Roberts, Labour; Clement Freud, Liberal; and Jo Richardson, Labour), along with the chairman of the British Youth Council (Peter Mandelson) and the director of the National Youth Bureau (David Howie). The main presentation was made by four teenagers (Russell Dexter, Helen McCormack, Tom Haworth and Jain Clarke).[243] Rose Robertson and Micky Burbidge also attended. Most of the MPs present were in favour of lowering the age of consent. Jo Richardson agreed to take up the matter with the Home Secretary.[244]

The Gay Youth Movement was established in England in 1980 as a national forum and network run by gay and lesbian young people to promote and assist gay youth groups and LGBT young people. GYM also ran a number of events for young LGBT people. Membership was open to individuals under 26. The setting of the age at 26 perhaps reflected the fact that many young gay people had delayed their sexual development by experiencing a suppressed teenagehood where there were no opportunities to express love and learn to love the people they wanted to. So it is understandable that many gay young people were only able to 'come out' when past their teens. Rather like special needs today, where young people are often allowed to remain in youth provision until aged 25.

The Gay Youth Movement was separate from the LGTG. It was a national organisation helping to promote gay youth groups and support gay young people. It organised gatherings and holidays. It ran a pen pal scheme. Those involved in running it tended to be very vocal, political, active and on the radical wing of gay politics. There was some crossover in membership with the LGTG and many former LGTG members went on to be active in GYM. But it is important to recognise that the LGTG and GYM were two very different organisations. LGTG was a youth club. Many in the LGTG had nothing to do with the GYM and many were put off by its political activity.

The archives disproportionately reflect those who were political activists. They were the ones who created news and produced magazines and articles. They were the ones on public marches. Just as gay history in the UK needs to recognise that only a very small proportion of gay men and woman ever had anything to do with CHE or the GLF, so most gay teenagers had no connection to the LGTG or the GYM. However, through the activities of the LGTG and GYM and the publicity they generated, many gay teenagers discovered a connection and a sense of not being alone.

The first conference of the GYM was held in London, 26–27 July 1980, with £100 being given by the National Association of Youth Clubs to help plan the conference.[245] The event was attended by approximately 80 young people.[246]

In July 1980 the *Birmingham Post* reported of plans to set up a gay youth group in Birmingham for young people aged between 13 and 21. Tom Haworth, age 19, said he hoped the group would meet at St Martin's Church in the Bull Ring and that a similar group would be established in Coventry.[247] The paper's editorial called on people to protest against such an idea: 'Most parents and any other responsible people will find the idea of a "gay" club for this age group outrageous'. This was followed by an article in the *Daily Telegraph* entitled 'Homosexuals plan club for boys in church hall; Thirteen-year-old boys are to be allowed to join a homosexual youth club, which, it is planned, will open in a church hall'.[248] The Birmingham group had not been set up by March 1981. At a meeting of the JCGT on 7 March 1981 in Manchester it was reported that 'Birmingham had not quite started due to worries around a member who took an overdose'. Minutes of the meeting state that the Birmingham group: 'aim to restart on 8th March. Will now meet with supervision as a safeguard and support'.[249]

Claire Rayner, who wrote a popular 'Agony Aunt' column in the *Sunday Mirror*, gave out the details of the JCGT, as well as Parents Enquiry, to one 17-year-old boy writing to her about the abuse he received at school for being out as gay.[250]

Richard Prout, an undergraduate at Queen Mary's College, London, studying English, was attending the LGTG around this time. Richard, who came from Forest Gate, London, was involved in organising the East London Gay Liberation Front, which was set up in March 1979.[251]

1980 was a busy year for young gay activists with many small developments throughout the country. Isolated individuals often found they had support, mainly from the JCGT and then the GYM.

Chapter Eight

Martin Collins explained his involvement in the LGTG:

Gary Barker, John Zold and myself hung around a lot doing stuff for the group, we even did a few editions of a little-known magazine as a rival to GYM magazine: ours was called *Pink Gym*, a photocopied thing on coloured paper, done by Gary as he worked for Islington Library and had free access to their Xerox copier.[252] We had cards with aliases: Gary Barker was Paul Baker, I (Martin Collins) was Mike Bull, John Zold was John Peterson I think. Gary got us backstage at *The Rocky Horror Show* for an interview with Riff Raff and Magenta. The group as you will know had a contact line, originally through the Manor Gardens Centre. But through a Greater London Council [GLC] grant, our own dedicated line was installed. There were various notes of what to say or not say to callers, rather jumbled, so with Chair's consent I bought stencils and created clear guidance on A3 card that went on the wall.

I also obtained a large scale map of London railways, the tube system and outer lying areas, as well as large scale of all of the London Transport bus network. These were fixed to a large swing-out board on the wall so that if a caller required directions, or the person on the phone wished to see roughly where said caller was travelling from, it was easier than 'where's the map gone?' I feel becoming Treasurer kinda excluded me from early sexual encounters with my peers because of an unwritten rule that group officers shouldn't have affairs with members. Maybe I hid behind this a little, but I also didn't go on some of the early trips or summer camps either. But equally I feel that I may have been happier at secondary school if I hadn't been aware of my sexuality to the extent that I was.

With Chris Heaume's input I applied twice to Capital Radio's 'Help a London Child' for group funding but failed because we did not have charitable status. The group started the LGTG Sponsorship Scheme which we gave out as we did fundraising pub crawls from Hampstead to Wimbledon.[253] From some application or other we got our own record player/cassette player/radio music centre, which Brian Earl [Manor Gardens Centre staff] got a lockable cabinet made for. I then used threaded bolt lengths and nuts to fix it so it couldn't go walkies, as we weren't the only group to use the Lecture Hall for meetings. We also got our own electronic typewriter and our own electric (!) Gestetner duplicator. I was one of a group of members who were asked to talk at a youth group, I think in Wimbledon, on a dark and windy, wet evening.

I went finally on a GYM Summer Camp near Scarborough which was fun[254].

In a two-page set of notes (no date) entitled 'London Gay Teenage Group – Notes on Fundraising' and signed 'Hope these notes are useful', Chris (Heaume) gives ideas for pub collections, club collections and raffles. The idea of teenagers going into pubs collecting money was not considered unusual then. Certainly no-one considered something like a risk assessment. Regarding pubs, two members would go in first to get permission to collect. The notes state: 'Collectors should be prepared to stand and chat, joke, explain about the group and what the money will be for, to the "punters"... Especially good clubs last year were: Bangs, Heaven. Good pubs: King William IV, Vauxhall Tavern, Queens' Head, Laurel Tree, Salisbury (But there are a lot of new ones opened since then)'.[255]

In April 1981 Jay McLaren, Kevin O'Neill and Gary Barker addressed all members of the LGTG in a letter appealing to them to think carefully about their behaviour at the group as it might affect newcomers:

In our relief at being able to mix with other gay people of similar ages, we all tend to act, speak and dress in a way which can be off-putting to newcomers, many of whom walk straight out or never attend another meeting. Members of the group, including ourselves, have always assumed that callers and new members immediately solve all their gay-related problems when they come to the group. This is obviously not the case at all... Those who are nervous or worried (as we must expect most to be) can be very put off by the 'screaming queen' sessions and pairs of members involved in heavy kissing, for example.[256]

The open letter also appeals to more members to get involved in organising events and activities.

At the end of May JCGT and GYM held a joint weekend workshop at Grapevine in London.[257]

Richard Desmond had joined the LGTG, aged 15, in 1979, while he was still at school in Bethnal Green. He became an activist. In 1981, when still aged 16, his case challenging the law on the age of consent was taken up by lawyers with a view of getting it into the European Court of Human Rights in Strasbourg as Anon v United Kingdom. The case did not reach the ECHR but was the first known attempt to raise the age of consent issue at that level. In 2020 Richard reflected on his relationship with Bob Webber, who he met at the LGTG:

I met Bob Webber on the Sunday before his 18th birthday in the garden [at Manor Gardens] sat on the bench, it changed my life. Today [7 June 2020] is the Sunday before what should have been his 56th birthday. I still have the slow burning rage that he's not here, he died in 1992. We were together 9 years and 9 months. He was the first person to love me unconditionally, looking back more than anything I'm grateful for what we had, two working class lads but from different parts of the City, we could only have met at LGTG.[258]

Richard was also volunteering at Gay Switchboard when only 16. He left Gay Switchboard but returned years later.[259]

Ash Kotak wrote in 2020:

I was 15 in 1981 when I had my first copy of *Gay News* which I had managed to get from a kiosk on Oxford Street near where my father's accountancy firm was situated. I knew I was gay from quite young, I had absolutely no interest in girls nor in dressing up in my mum's saris.

I needed to find other people like me so when I saw the advert for the London Gay Teenage Group, I thought I would go along. I was excited with all the passion of a blossoming teenager with a permanent hard on. The idea of sex with someone my age or someone older was exciting – I had already been experimenting with a mate at school since the age of 12. Albeit in retrospect now, it was quite abusive, I've grown to understand it from his side.

Most of my mates at school were already dating and spent half their time snogging their girlfriends on the bus, in the street, in the playground, at parties, and at the roller disco at the Electric Ballroom in Camden Town which a bunch of us frequented. Life was easy for my mates and I wanted the same thing.

I took the 134 bus to Archway Station one sunny May afternoon, and walked the short distance to Manor Gardens off the Holloway Road wearing black stay-press trousers (which the mods and skins wore), white socks, white Adidas Gazelles, white t shirt and a legendary too-big-for-my-short-skinny-frame, burgundy, waffle-knit, button-front Relco cardigan (all bought from Edmonton Market), with a classic sideways fringed wedge hairstyle. I was a Soul-boy but dressed like a Mod because most of my mates were Mods.

I stood outside for what felt like an age staring at a single-storey hut situated in a garden which looked quite out of place with its surroundings. I hadn't worked out what I'd do post the dressing up, sneaking out of home and the journey here. I walked up and down the road with a hard on desperate for a wank. It was that which gave me the guts to walk in. I froze and everyone ignored me. There were heaps of people around, of all colours, just like Petticoat Lane Market where I'd go buy the latest 12 inches to play at a mate's soul parties in Barnet. I knew I looked young. A group of lads, everyone was so tall, chased a blond kid from the room I was in at the right, past the entrance to another room on the other side – 'Let's all strip him and rape him.' They all screamed and wolf whistled. These were not at all how I imagined gays to be! We are meant to be sensitive, caring, friendly, horny yes and ordinary mostly to fit in. I had already read *The Naked Civil Servant* from my local library and there were a couple of gay stories in the *Hammer House of Horror* series and I'd been obsessed with the Jeremy Thorpe and Norman Scott trial of 1979, my early wanking days. Should I leave or stay? I was scared. A hot man with an American accent came over and introduced himself as Gregg. 'I've been to America,' I tried. 'I'm Canadian,' he answered. I went quiet and Gregg rushed off. 'Guys settle down!' A blond guy who seemed to be a leader too came over. 'Hi, I'm Chris. Don't worry about them, it's not always like this.' All I could think of was did they spot my hard on. It was the beginning of my gay life.[260]

Gavin Simmons recalled:

I first went to LGTG in September, I think it was '81, year of the royal wedding [Prince Charles and Diana Spencer]! I was 19 and just moved to London to do a year's work experience. I'm fairly sure Manor Gardens was the first ever gay place I went to, I got the details from Switchboard. Looking back it was a positive experience and the group provided a safe place to take my very first steps. I went to the GYM-LGTG camp in Sheffield in 82 and the two following camps, Scarborough 83 and Aberystwyth 84.[261]

Gavin's personal story appeared in Norris and Read's book *Out* (1985) under the name Martin. He also appeared as David in *Just Seventeen* magazine.[262]

In *Out* (1985) Gavin explained that he made a note of the Gay Switchboard number but that it took some time 'to summon up the courage' to ring them. 'I'd ring the number and then put the phone down, and if it was engaged, I'd think, "oh good". Then suddenly it rang; it was answered quickly and I just sort of froze for a second'. Martin was given information of organisations that might be helpful. The call put Martin into an 'emotional high'. The book goes on to describe how nervous Martin was when he first approached the LGTG. 'I was absolutely petrified; I just didn't know what to expect. I felt it was the biggest thing I'd ever done. I walked in and there were two rooms; the first room had a pool table and music playing, like a youth club. I suppose there must have been about ten or fifteen punky-looking people in there, just playing pool and chatting. They just looked up as I came in and looked away again. I wasn't sort of mobbed or anything'. Martin went back and gradually got to know people at the group. He goes on to describe the excitement of his first gay disco and gay sex. And the nice time he had the second time he had sex, until he found out he had contracted NSU (non-specific urethritis).

From June 1981 the JCGT and GYM worked together to produce *Gay Youth*, a magazine. This ran to over 20 issues, but issues after 1982 were produced by GYM alone and the tone and format of the magazine changed significantly. *Gay Youth* was like the GLF's *Come Together*, with no rules about editorial or how it was put together.[263] Issue 1 (June 1981) mentions that the LGTG management committee were hoping to get their own part-time paid youth worker (this happened the following year). Page 2 also reports that the LGTG reluctantly banned a 14-year-old boy from attending (ILEA conditions required the group to operate a strict 16–21 age group policy). While this sounds negative and cold it followed long debates with the Islington Youth Officer Ray Walker. The group risked losing its status and support as an official youth club if it knowingly allowed under-16-year-olds to attend. In 1981 two documented complaints were received by Islington Youth Service regarding under-16-year-old children attending the group. Both Winston Pinder (Islington Youth Service) and Ray Walker had to remind the group of the need to strictly adhere to the age restrictions.[264] The LGTG survived largely through the support of Islington Youth Service and would have been unlikely to have survived in many other London boroughs. The issue of under-16-year-olds attending was often raised, particularly in 1985 and 1986. It was partially resolved when Ray Walker was able to establish a statutory service (North London Line) which could absorb the 'risk' of young people under 16 more easily than a voluntary youth club like LGTG.

Issue 1 of *Gay Youth* also reports on some gay youth groups outside London. In Southampton we read that the group, which has close ties with the Women's Centre, emerged at the same time as the GaySoc collapsed. Vincent Knight-Newbury was involved in Southampton CHE, the Southampton Gay Youth Group and GaySoc, and helped to make the Southampton Youth Group very active and organised.[265] In addition, Vincent helped put together the first issues of *Gay Youth*. The March meeting of the JCGT held in Manchester had updates from Birmingham, London, Manchester, Bradford and Stoke, where the youth group had collapsed.[266]

Issue 2 of *Gay Youth* reports on new gay youth groups in Derby, Lewisham and Guildford. The Lewisham Group, known as the South London Gay Young People's Group, for 16- to 21-year-olds, met on Mondays in Catford and Keith Trotman was involved in that.[267] *Gay Youth* also reported that Tom Haworth had been appointed to the CHE executive committee with special responsibility for gay youth.

In July 1981 there were riots in Britain, and many parts of inner London boarded up their shop-fronts to prevent them from getting smashed. The author recalls going to the Movements Disco at the Carved Red Lion near Islington Green, and seeing lots of boarded-up shop-fronts and vans full of police officers as he made his way there from the Angel. It was also at the Carved Red Lion disco that the author witnessed Jimmy Somerville attacking a young man and women who were dancing together at the pub, shouting, 'Get

74

out, straights!' at them. Such a separatist attitude was alarming to the author. And on reflection, the couple could anyway have been bisexuals or just gay and lesbian friends.

On 7 August 1981 Gary Barker, chair of LGTG, resigned to go travelling round Europe.

In August the LGTG featured in *Capital Gay* with a photo of Derek, Shimon and Max. The report explains that the group was run by its members and that as Chris Heaume (volunteer youth worker) remarked: 'they are responsible for all their own successes and failures'. The group was reported to receive 40–50 phone calls a week and that the teenagers, after training, answered the calls. Ten members of the group went to a conference on minorities in Germany in June 1981 the paper reported.[268] In August 1981 some LGTG members attended GayFest in Durham. It was at GayFest that the GYM held its first AGM. Richard Desmond, a LGTG member, was appointed coordinator; Vincent Knight (also known as Knight-Newbury) secretary, and Lyn Thomas treasurer.[269] GYM membership was about 200 in 1982. At a meeting of the JCGT on 30 August 1982 a decision was made by that group to allow all of its work to be absorbed by GYM and for GYM to stand alone and be run by young people.[270]

Issues of *Gay Youth* after 1981 often contained support for the Paedophile Information Exchange (PIE). Issue 4 (1981/2) had an article explaining what PIE was and stated 'Paedophile love is as natural as parental love … We campaign for the legal and social acceptance of paedophilia'. The magazine went on: 'that it is unjust to children to outlaw their sexuality'.

Issue 6 (August–September 1982) revealed who the editors of *Gay Youth* were: Vincent Knight (previously known as Knight-Newbury), Jay McLaren and Sarah Green.

Issue 10 (December 1983/January 1984) reaffirmed 'GYM supports paedophiles'. The front page of this issue reported on an impending prosecution of three members of PIE on charges relating to a publication called 'Contact'. On page seven of issue 10, Tom of GYM, in reply to a letter from National Friend, states 'We as young gay people reject anti-paedophile laws in the same way as we reject the male under 21 law'. He then goes on to say: 'In no way is paedophile love "sinister". Paedophile relationships are based on free and happy consent of both partners and so should be supported and encouraged'.

The existence of this material in the archives now presents a safeguarding issue for archivists. A visit by young people in 2018 to the HCA to view gay youth material resulted in a careful selection of the items on display. This particular aspect of the chapter of gay youth activism is one that many would rather forget. Very few young people today would advocate free sexual relations between adults and children under 16, and if they did the law could fall very heavily upon them. The small minority of gay people who supported PIE were like many other activists, disproportionately represented in publicity and media. And their support for paedophilia only reinforced prejudices about gay men being a danger to children.

In September *Capital Gay* reviewed the JCGT publication *Breaking the Silence*.[271] 'A book written by gay teenagers and believed to be the first of its kind in the world is being published in London on Monday', the review started. Co-author Jonathan Walters said: 'We wanted to let young people speak for themselves rather than interpose our views'. The review prints the story of Derek, 18, Streatham, one of over 30 young people whose stories are in the book: 'I went to a gay youth club once but that wasn't any good. I was the only one from south London there and besides, they were a load of fucking poufs, all trying to act like women and that sort of stuff. What's the point in that? I like blokes because they are blokes not because they're like women'.

I can only imagine Derek attended the LGTG at a session dominated by loud camp 'queens' (an issue which the group tried to address once or twice when the LGTG committee realised it was off-putting to many newcomers).

Breaking the Silence contained the stories of 34 gay and lesbian young people. The individual accounts were collected in 1979 from around the country by people in contact with gay teenagers. The appendix lists 25 groups associated with the JCGT and final page has useful contact numbers.

On Wednesday 9 September 1981 the AGM of the LGTG was held at Manor Gardens. Jain Clarke was unanimously elected as chair.[272] It was noted that some over-21-year-olds had still been attending the group. The meeting agreed on a blanket ban on all 'persons over the age of 21' except those on the management committee. As a consequence, Andrew Martin was to hand his keys in until 'such time as he can officially attend meetings as a MC member'. Jain Clarke subsequently wrote to Andrew Martin asking him if he would like to join the MC.[273] It is thought that Andrew Martin did not join the committee and thus ended his long involvement in the group. Incidentally the group was originally intended to be for under-21-year-olds, but many of the subsequent documents refer to the issue of people over the age of 21 in the group. Thus there is at times some ambiguity about persons aged 21 in the group. However, at the AGM in October 1983 when the constitution of the group was passed, it states under 'Membership': 'Membership of the group shall be open to people between the ages of 16 and 21 years old, regardless of sex or sexuality. No-one who has reached their twenty-first birthday may remain or become a member of the group'. The original constitution when the group registered with ILEA in 1979 stated 'Membership of the group shall be open to young people between the ages of 16–21 years old, whether they be homosexual, heterosexual or bisexual'.[274]

The management committee meeting on 5 October reported that Jay, Martin and the area youth officer had met and discussed conditions for the group before a youth worker could be allocated. The roles of Chris Heaume, Jane Dixon and Gilly Salvat were briefly discussed. Clarification of the conditions was to be sought from the area youth officer. The meeting also noted that Jonathan Walters would approach Angus Hamilton to see if he would be the group's solicitor.[275] The 9 November meeting records that Mark Ashton attended as the representative of Gay Switchboard. Switchboard and CHE were invited to send representatives after the meeting in September agreed that they should be part of the management committee, along with London Friend.

In November 1981 *Kicks*, a new teenage magazine, published by Teenage Kicks Ltd, mentions the Gay Teenage Group in their contacts page on 'Gays'.[276]

GYM/JCGT held a weekend workshop in Liverpool, 21–22 November 1981, along with the AGM of JCGT.[277] It was noted at the AGM that over 1,000 copies of *Breaking the Silence* had been sold. And the publication *I know what I am* was now out of print. A further 500 copies of the latter book were to be printed. Four new gay youth groups were noted in Bristol, Leicester, South London and Coppull, near Preston.[278]

Chapter Nine

A FIRST: PAID PART-TIME YOUTH WORKERS
FOR GAY TEENAGERS, 1982

The Young Lesbian Group broke away from the LGTG to form part of the Camden and Islington Girls Project. This was for funding reasons. Camden Young Lesbians met at 4 Caversham Road, Kentish Town. Sessions included a visit from Jane Lethbridge of Grapevine, exploring the female anatomy.[279] The Islington Girls Project was based at Manor Gardens and the Young Lesbian Group met on Monday evenings.

In February two part-time youth worker posts were advertised for the LGTG and the Young Lesbian Group to be paid for by ILEA (Inner London Education Authority). Seven hours per week was allocated to LGTG and three and a half to the Young Lesbian Group as part of the Islington Girls Project. Adverts were placed with a closing date of 5 February.

Lawrie Norcross, headmaster of Highbury Grove School and executive member of the National Association of Schoolmasters and Union of Women Teachers, objected and thought it 'extraordinary to be spending money on an exercise of dubious morality and possible dubious legality'. He stated:

> If money was going to be spent on homosexuals I would far rather it is spent on medical and psychiatric counselling than on bringing them together in groups reinforcing their abnormality and giving institutional backing to it.[280]

The Nationwide Festival of Light, a Christian morality campaign which had objected to the registration of the group in 1979, wrote to the director of ILEA questioning the recruitment of youth workers to lead teenage lesbian and homosexual groups. In their letter they ask: 'whether the counselling given by a salaried leader of a homosexual youth group would aim to release youngsters from involvement with homosexual practices, or whether it would be to confirm them in such practices and to encourage in the idea that such a way of life is natural and normal for them'.[281] I think the answer to that question is pretty obvious!

Harry Greenway, Member of Parliament for Ealing, took up the issue in the House of Commons. On 1 February he 'asked the Secretary of State for Education and Science if he will use his powers under the Education Act 1944 to direct any local authority which maintains youth clubs run for homosexuals below the age of consent to cease to do so; and if he will make a statement'. William Sheldon, Parliamentary Under-Secretary of State for Education, replied: 'My right hon. Friend is investigating reports that the ILEA is supporting work with groups of young homosexuals. He will reach a view on what action should be taken in the light of the facts established. I will write to my hon. Friend to convey the outcome'.[282]

On 5 February 1982 the Islington newspaper reports on the use of public funds to pay for youth workers at a gay teenage and young lesbian group, the negative criticism of a gay teenage and young lesbian group, the use of public funds and the reasoning by the Inner London Education Authority (ILEA) for approving the application.[283] *Capital Gay* reported 'Tories fail to halt the grants' on its front page of 19 February 1982. A grant of £1,000 to the LGTG was agreed and £4,315 to London Friend. Other grants were made to Lesbian Line and A Woman's Place.

'Gay Teenagers are Everywhere', a poster produced by the JCGT, was distributed to youth clubs.[284] The Manchester Gay Youth Group was flourishing by 1982. Meeting on Saturday afternoons at the council-funded gay centre in Bloom Street, the group featured in *Gay News* in March 1982. 'Kevin is 19. When he realised he was gay a year ago, he told his mother Joyce, and she encouraged him to come to the club ... Joyce is the only parent who is really involved in the club but acts like a mum for all the young people'.[285]

With Gregg Blachford's arrival at the LGTG in March 1982, as a paid part-time youth worker, a new element of politics was introduced to group sessions.[286] Political awareness very much rooted in Gregg's own roots in the GLF (in Australia) and Gay Left in London. Some attendees did not like this. Gregg was working at Paddington College when he had the part-time job with the LGTG at Manor Gardens.[287] In 2021 Gregg gave an interview to Eleanor Affleck as part of the Museum of Youth Culture 'Growing up Queer' collection.[288] In that interview Gregg explained how he was employed for seven hours per week at the LGTG; three on a Wednesday evening and four on Sunday afternoon. Gregg stated that the group was very youth driven and run by the young people. Although made welcome by the group, Gregg was told, 'We don't want adults coming in to tell us what to do' and 'You're here to do activities, you are not here to lead the group'. The ethos of a youth led group was not going to be lost just because ILEA had decided the group should have a youth worker.

Gregg describes the two rooms at Manor Gardens; one with louder people (smoke, billiards, raucous behaviour) and a quieter one (non-smoking, discussion). The latter room allowed newcomers to feel at ease and be made welcome. The confident noisy young gay guys in the first room could be quite off-putting and frightening for many who were at a gay venue for the first time in their life.

In July 1982, Owen, Wayne [Shires] and Stephen featured in *Gay News*, 'average age 18 going on 19, living in a squat in Shaftesbury Avenue'. Owen stated he used to be a regular at the Gay Teenage Group but stopped going:

> ... when they started making it so serious, with boring lectures. The people there now take it too seriously, they try too hard. If a very young gay person went there for the first time they'd probably be bored stiff with all that talk about sexism and racism. Nobody talks about their own lives there. It should be social and have more counselling services and things like that.[289]

In May 1982 the Labour Party won 51 out of 52 seats on Islington Borough Council. And the one seat they failed to win was lost by one vote. Many moderate members of the party had left to join the Liberal/SDP alliance and so the left wing dominated the party that was left after the 'defections'. Labour in Islington then started to support and promote many, for the time, radically left policies; setting up a Gay and Lesbian Working Party, flying the red flag from the council building, ploughing money into women's groups, gay groups and black groups. Motions passed by the council included a ban on Irish jokes and a call for the withdrawal of troops from Northern Ireland.[290] Islington became the focus of much newspaper attention. Out of step with its traditional voters, in the next round of council elections, in 1986, they lost a lot of seats to Liberal/Social Democratic Party candidates but managed to hold on to overall control of the council.

The LGTG Annual Report 1982 contains a piece by chairperson Jain Clarke. She points out that the average stay for a member in the group is three to five months, causing much fluctuation, that the group relies on a few members who attend regularly, and that a part-time youth worker was recently appointed (Gregg Blachford). The annual report goes on to give a history of the group and cites it as launching itself in February 1976 when 'it had been invited to use the premises of Grapevine in Holloway Road ... had designed its own logo, printed its letterheads, scrounged a record player, advertised its phone number and was springing away from the starting blocks'.[291] In September 1979 the group had grown to 50 on Sundays and 20 on Wednesday evenings. On page 14 of the annual report a few of the newspaper headlines and quotes from politicians following funding from the GLC are given: 'Teenagers will be corrupted rather than helped by an organisation such as this'.[292]

The draft constitution drawn up in 1982 states that the 'aim of the Group will be to help its members gain a positive view of themselves and so develop their physical, educational, mental and social capacities that they may grow fully as individuals and members of society and that their conditions of life may be improved'.

The document also states that the membership of the group shall be open to people between the ages of 16 and 21 years old, regardless of sex and sexuality. No-one who has reached their twenty-first birthday may retain or become a member of the group.[293] It is clear that some young people did remain in the group after they became 21. There was no requirement for attendees to register with their date of birth. Some people looked younger than 21 when they were in fact over 21. In some cases when members became 21 they were able to stay on at the group by becoming members of the management committee.[294]

The support and involvement of Friend in the LGTG is mentioned. Philip Conn from Friend sat on the management committee and many referrals came from Friend. The LGTG also benefited from Friend's specialist training and knowledge on transsexualism and transvestism.[295]

Other members of the management committee included: Brian Earl (Manor Gardens Centre), David Bell (Beauchamp Lodge), Jonathan Walters, Jay McLaren and Mark Ashton (London Gay Switchboard).[296]

London Gay Switchboard and *Gay News* were the main places that attendees of the LGTG found out about the group in the first place.

The GYM London Conference 'Pride and Prejudice' was held in spring 1982. Sixty-nine people officially registered for the conference, almost half of them unemployed. Discussion groups looked at 'the role of GYM, feminism, coming out, paedophilia, promiscuity and how gay youth groups can increase their support for each other'.[297]

In May 1982 GYM published its Gay Youth Charter. It starts 'Gay Liberation requires the liberation of all other oppressed groups including sexual minorities such as transsexuals, transvestites and paedophiles, and this requires a society where all forms of consensual sexual activity are regarded as equally valid'. It included an end to the age of consent (that is, no age of consent), money and facilities for gay youth groups, the right to be adopted or fostered as openly gay and the right to adopt or foster others, and the abolition of privileges for heterosexual couples.[298] CHE discussed the charter at their annual conference in Sheffield. CHE supported the general aims of GYM but could not endorse the charter, in particular the reference to support for paedophiles.[299]

The British Library has recordings of pirate radio programme from 1982 called 'Gaywaves'. One of the recordings is of a visit to the LGTG, broadcast 21 July 1982 and 28 July 1982. Philip Cox and Annabelle visited the LGTG and spoke to Claude, Robert and Mike. They reported that there were about 40 young people at the group that afternoon. The place filled up at about 4.30pm and there was noise, table tennis and music. Also included in the Gaywaves recording is a brief interview with Simon Baldwin about a meeting at County Hall. David Beck also reports on the National Association of Youth Clubs Conference. Claude, Robert and Mike may be fictional names used?[300] A broadcast on 1 September 1982 gives an account by Martin (no surname given) who had a negative experience at the GYM summer camp near Sheffield. He left early.

Four members of the LGTG (Carl Spurling, Paul Gleghorn, Simon Shipman and David Beck, two of whom were also in the GYM) attended the NAYC Annual Conference at Warwick University in July 1982. Gregg Blachford drove the minibus and on his return to London immediately started a night shift at Switchboard.

Marc Burke joined the LGTG in 1982 and remained a member until about 1984. He had joined the Metropolitan Police cadets in 1981 and stayed in the police until 1986. As such, he was probably the only gay police officer who was in the group at the same time as being in the police: a fact that he must have kept secret from his police colleagues. Later he studied being gay in the police force, wrote a thesis on the subject and published an important book.[301] In 2020 Marc reflected on how finding the LGTG might have saved his life, although his first visit to the group was almost his last on account of the dominance of screaming queens:

Back in the 80s, I was pretty close to being another gay suicide statistic: a gay Metropolitan Police officer struggling with a conservative upbringing and religious confusion. A tough, judo black belt police officer by day, pathetic, pending suicide casualty by night. A double life where I was doing a miserable job of fitting into either category. And there was no resolution in sight. Well, almost none.

I first learned about the London Gay Teenage Group on LBC [London Broadcasting Company]'s Nightline show with Adrian Love. They had a gay segment and would often provide useful support numbers over the air. I felt that what was going on in my brain could no longer be written off as a 'phase', but the last thing I wanted to do was go to a gay group. But alone in my room, I'd suffered enough suicidal ideation to know that I had to make a choice: find this group and figure things out, or jump off one of the new M25 overpasses that had recently begun to weave its way through sleepy Surrey.

I eventually plucked up the courage to make the trek to north London, only to find the group was every bit as awful as I expected it to be. Populated by flamboyant drama queens with whom I had nothing in common, I remember wanting to leave the moment I arrived. I wanted nothing to do with them. Dejected, I returned home to spend another month of evenings quietly alone in my room. By now the M25 had already reached Reigate.

Eventually, I returned. Not because I wanted to, but because I had to. After all, there were a couple of guys there who seemed pretty 'normal'. I could just hang out with them, right?

Making those first couple of friends turned out to be key. And so my recovery began. It was a slow process that led me to ditch all religions entirely.[302]

In September 1982 *Capital Gay* reported that the South London Gay Young People's Group celebrated its first year with a birthday party. Twenty people turned up.[303] Outside of London there was a Gay Youth Group in Southampton which met on Sundays. The group was for under-26-year-olds and produced their own magazine called *Jeune*, edited by Mark Ovenden and Karl Lewis.[304] The LGTG £1,000 fund appeal was running in September 1982. The fundraising was for a letter-writing campaign (letters to go to every school in London), to support young people with travel expenses to GYM and NAYC conferences, and to fund a library for the group.[305] A talk at Hampstead CHE led to a donation by that group of £40.[306] A jumble sale was held at 6 Manor Gardens on 25 September, which raised over £100.[307]

Around 1982 there was an incident regarding a 14- or 15-year-old boy who ran off to Amsterdam and was threatening to contact the *News of the World* and say that he had been sent there by the LGTG to be a prostitute in the city. He was a regular at Piccadilly Circus Station (subway 4 was famous for rent boys) and thought he could do better in Amsterdam.[308] Jonathan Walters dashed off to Amsterdam, found the boy and brought him back before any harm was done. Apparently the management committee of the LGTG were not impressed that they had not been told about this event until after Jonathan had left for Amsterdam. Of course the group did not officially allow under-16s to attend, but occasionally they might turn up and sometimes pretend to be 16 or older. Identification documents were not required. The issue of under-16-year-olds at the group was a reoccurring issue which later was to threaten loss of official registration and financial support.

Jay McLaren and Paul Thurlow of the GYM spoke at the Labour Party Conference.[309] Paul appeared on the front cover of the *Mancunian Gay*.

True Romance Etc, a short film on the BFI website, has the Gay Switchboard number listed at the end of the film for details of 'gay teenager groups'. The film features a handful of openly gay teenagers. The film was released in 1982. Camden Girls Project are listed in the credits.[310] The October 1982 issue of *HIM Monthly* featured an article on Gregg Blachford and the gay youth movement:

It's always been a strong principle of the group, and of the few adults associated with it, that the LGTG should be run by the members … Some members are extrovert and they do camp around. They don't like taking part in 'serious' conversations about the group and they call other members 'square'. They can be a bit disruptive, especially when the group holds its monthly meetings. They can also put new people off because the flamboyant ones are the most visible and they seem to reinforce stereotypes about gay people.[311]

The photo that had appeared of group members in *Mister* in 1980 was republished with the article about Gregg Blachford.

Over the weekend of 12–14 November 1982 some 15 members of the LGTG stayed at Chequer Cottage, Stadhampton, Oxfordshire. The purpose of the weekend, as well as having fun, was 'to look at the past achievements of the group and to plan future events and to look at how the group is/should be operating.'[312]

In November 1982 *Capital Gay* announced that the LGTG had been awarded a grant of £13,994 for the following year by the GLC. The same month saw AIDS reported in *Capital Gay* with a headline 'US disease hits London'.[313] The disease had actually arrived months earlier but little was known and it spread undetected. Awareness and knowledge of AIDS throughout the early 1980s was very sketchy and there were a lot of rumours and a lack of clear understanding of exactly how it was caught. The term AIDS was first coined in July 1982.[314]

In December 1982 the group submitted a report to the 'Experience and Participation; Review Group on the Youth Service in England' (known as 'the Thompson report'). The group's response was written by Gregg Blachford and Chris Heaume. While welcoming the Youth Service report they were disappointed that it made no reference to gay young people and that gay youth groups had not been consulted. The LGTG response was taken up by the Chair of ILEA's Further and Higher Education Sub Committee, Neil Fletcher. He called a group of people together to see what the ILEA youth service could do to help gay teenagers.[315]

A Christmas party was held on Saturday 18 December at Manor Gardens.

Chapter Ten

'RATES CASH FOR GAY TEENAGERS' ROW, 1983

The GLC grant of over £13,000 to the LGTG was to enable the group to employ two part-time research workers. This caused some headline news and objections, and in the summer was cited as a good reason, along with funding for other 'wacky causes', to abolish the GLC.

In February LGTG were seeking office space near Holloway Road for the research project.[316] Offices were rented in Camden. On 16 March Hugh Warren, aged 22, and Lorraine Trenchard, aged 25, started work on GLC-funded research by LGTG, to assess the needs of gay youth in London. This was a pioneering piece of work.[317] A committee was formed by the LGTG to oversee the project and Martin Collins dealt with the accounts. The first publication from the researchers came the following year (see Chapter Eleven, 1984). Lorraine Trenchard also helped out at the Young Lesbian Group. She recalled, 'I joined the YLG as a voluntary youth worker. I was about 25 – so the top end of the age group. I never attended as just a member. Jane Dixon, Jane Skeats and Gilly Salvat were the real pioneers.'[318]

In 1983 the secretary of the GYM, Paul Thurlow, addressed the British Youth Council. At that time the GYM had 'visitor' status at the British Youth Council.

Early in the year GYM took a delegation to Parliament. Thirty or more young gays meet 12 MPs at the House of Commons. The MPs included Jo Richardson (Labour), Clement Freud (Liberal) and Martin Stevens (Conservative). Stevens was a vice-president of CHE but seemed opposed to lowering the age of consent from 21 (angering the delegation) and causing an issue for CHE. However, the 50-minute meeting in Committee Room 16 was considered a 'success' by Paul Thurlow of GYM.[319]

GAY YOUTH GROUPS

STARTING YOUR OWN STARTING YOUR OWN STARTIN
TING YOUR OWN STARTING YOUR OWN STARTING YO
OWN STARTING YOUR OWN STARTING YOUR OWN ST
STARTING YOUR OWN STARTING YOUR OWN STARTIN

Social Issues   Personal Politics   Counselling and Personal Relationships

friends   Grants and Funding

GAY LIFE

Training   Gay politics   Education   dancing

Community Action

Groups and Groupwork   GAY TEENAGERS   Disco Music

Feminism   Leisure

Sexual Politics   THE GAY YOUTH MOV

llea

Education Officer P J Newsam MA

Islington Area Youth Office
White Lion Youth Centre
White Lion Street London N1 9PW

Mr A Martin,
London Gay Teenage Group,
9, Maria Gardens,
London N.7

Telephone 01 239 1807
Please reply to the Area Youth Officer
My reference
Your reference GA/RJ
Date 26/9/79

Dear Mr Martin,

I am pleased to inform you that the I.L.E.A. Youth Committee for Islington at its meeting on 11th September approved your application for Registration. I enclose a grant-aid handbook for your information.

Yours sincerely,

R. Joseph
(Clerical Officer)
G. Abbott (Mrs)
ADMINISTRATIVE OFFICER

P.S. Please note that the committee requested alteration of Nos 11 + 12 of your constitution. Either discuss this with Chris Heaume or phone me if you're not clear what I mean! R Abbott

21

22

23

Something to tell you brother. Darling, I have something to tell you. Something to tell you Sir. Doctor, I have something to tell you. Grandad, something to tell you. Lover, I have something to tell you. Something to tell you, friends. We have something to tell you, Miss. I have something to tell you. Something to tell you, mate. Uncle, I have something to tell you.

Something to tell you

Lorraine Trenchard & Hugh Warren

Talking about
SCHOOL

Hugh Warren
LONDON GAY TEENAGE GROUP

Talking about
YOUNG
LESBIANS

Edited by
Lorraine Trenchard
LONDON GAY TEENAGE GROUP

Talking about
YOUTH
WORK

Lorraine Trenchard
& Hugh Warren
LONDON GAY TEENAGE GROUP

24

25

gay teenage group
272 5741

Produced by young gays for young gays

Visions 25p

THE MAGAZINE OF THE L.G.T.G.

LGTG WILL BE 10 YEARS OLD THIS YEAR !!

INTO '86!

Happy Birthday To Us!

RUM, SODOMY AND THE CASH..!   PAGE 6-7

GIVING AND RECIEVING   PAGE 4

10TH ANNIVERSARY CELEBRATIONS!   PAGE 5

HAPPILY EVER AFTER... PAGE 3

25p

BADGE MAKING

Wearing a badge identifying yourself as gay or gay-friendly was an important part of 'coming out' and solidarity. The LGTG borrowed a badge-making machine and was able to make unique badges. Former members of the LGTG recalled memories of badges and badge making:

'Am I remembering correctly that one of our activities at one point in time was making badges with a machine someone had brought in?' Gregg Blachford.

The 'badge maker was probably on loan from community resource Islington Bus Company, near the junction of Liverpool Road and Holloway Road N7.' Martin Collins.[320]

'I remember the badge machine we had to loan from Islington resource centre. Was always stabbing myself in the hand with those pins!' Steve Lunniss.

'Wow – memories! The best one I ever saw was "Sodom Today, Gomorrah the World!"' Jon Pyper.[321]

'The "I'm a Nancy boy" [badge] one was my creation! I would put it at 1982, 1983 at the very latest.' David Joad.

'I was on the 82 and 83 Pride committee. The 82 badge was designed by David (Wilson-Carr?) and was seen as radical because it was square. The 83 badge was different because it was moulded plastic and not a classic metal based, pressed badge.' Jon Pyper.

BERMONDSEY AND BODY PARTS

In February 1983 mud-slinging was evident in the Bermondsey by-election, where Peter Tatchell, the Labour candidate, was the subject of homophobic abuse and ridicule. Labour lost the traditionally very safe Labour seat to the Liberals. Body parts were being discovered in North London at homes occupied by Denis Nilsen. Nilsen, it transpired, had met and murdered several young men. Nilsen was charged on 11 February 1983. One of his victims was described as an 18-year-old blue-eyed Scot who wore a green tracksuit top. Nilsen met him in The Golden Lion in 1981. This victim's identity was never established. A victim of Nilsen could have even attended the LGTG. We will never know. And did some young gay men who found a safe haven in the LGTG avoid falling into the clutches of Nilsen, or less dangerous older gay men?

From March 25–27 1983 the GYM event at Manor Gardens was called

'GYM'LL FIX IT': 'For Lesbians and gay men under 26'.[322] Photos at the Bishopsgate Institute show the programme and some attenders, including for 'Any Questions?': Paul Crane (lawyer), Bob Crossman (councillor), Jeffrey Weeks (historian), Peter Bradley (teacher), David Howie (National Youth Bureau), Bryn Davies (ILEA), Jan Parker (*Spare Rib* magazine), Frances Morrell (ILEA/GLC) and Linda Semple (*Gay News* 'Visible Lesbian'). Kenneth Williams and Claire Rayner had also been invited.[323] Lyn Thomas recalls supplying Frances Morrell with wine and making her feel more at ease. The play *Barriers* was performed by the LGTG with Jain Clarke, Carl Spurling and Steve Lunniss amongst the cast. Carl Spurling wrote and directed *Barriers*.

Following the production of *Barriers* seven people met at Carl Spurling's home in Bexleyheath on 30 May 1983 and set up 'The Homo Thespians', a young gay drama group for people aged between 16 and 25. As well as drama, the group organised social events. On Saturday 23 July 1983 they enjoyed a picnic in Knole Park, Kent.[324]

On 4 May 1983 15 LGTG members visited Ashburton Youth Club, London, SW15. There they met about 40–50 young people, mostly in the 15–16-year age group. After a bit of giggling from the Ashburton young people, the LGTG members went on to describe what the group was about and a useful discussion and question session followed.

Jon Pyper who lived at 14 Caledonian Road, otherwise known as the 'Wee Nooke', was aged 25 in 1983 and was active in GYM.[325] In 2019 Jon recalled:

It was a flat on three floors above a run-down TV repair shop, its front door hidden away behind an ancient, dusty, decrepit shop-front. However, for a while during the early 80s, its threshold was criss-crossed by many an LLGTG and LGYM member... Mark [Ashton], myself and Jimmy Somerville could often be found drinking coffee in Gay's the Word bookshop. Young, radical, political and in your face, we would sit there putting the world to rights, until we were told rather curtly that if we wished to scream our tits off, we could go elsewhere. I think it was a class thing! Around that time, Jimmy lived in a squat in Coptic Street, opposite the British Museum. He always seemed to have a pan of home-made soup on the go, and swore by its restorative powers in the face of all ills. Anyhow, Richard Coles and I were the founding fathers of Wee Nooke. Toby Kettle lived there for a while, as well as Jay McLaren and Tomas Busse. Visitors were numerous – not only Mark and Jimmy, but also Jonathan Walters, Roy Puddefoot,

Martin Collins, Lyn Thomas, Royce Ullah, and Rose Collis, to name but a few – and of course the one and only Steve Lunniss.[326]

During Lesbian and Gay Pride week both the LGTG and GYM were present with banners on the parade held on 2 July, with an estimated crowd of 2,000 people.[327] The LGTG got a mention in Parliament on 1 July in a debate about London. Sir George Young said in the House of Commons:

Our money has been invested in such projects as Babies against the Bomb, the English Collective of Prostitutes, the London Gay Teenage Group and the provision of crèches for the ladies of Greenham Common... For some time there have been good practical reasons for abolishing the GLC... the antics of Ken Livingstone and his colleagues have ensured that a strong intellectual case now commands widespread support.[328]

Not all news in the mainstream media was negative. *The Sun* newspaper on 1 August 1983 had a full-page spread: 'My son is gay; report on the shock fact that many parents face... I must tell you Mum. I fancy boys'. The piece featured Joyce Waite and her 20-year-old son Kevin. The article reported how supportive Joyce had become and that she helped at a gay centre in Manchester.[329] Kevin told his mum when he was 16. The address for Parents Enquiry was given and the telephone number for the Albany Trust.

Christopher Rossmanith-Shoulder, as he is now known, used to go to the Tyneside Gay Teenage Group in the early '80s and also attended the 1983 and 1984 GYM summer camps. The Tyneside Gay Teenage Group was formed in 1980 by Newcastle Friend. Chris recalled:

TGTG met on a Friday evening in a room in St Andrew's church in the centre of Newcastle, from about 7pm until 10 pm. It was made up of teenage boys mostly and perhaps the odd girl. Anywhere between 5 to 15 people attending. Our ages ranged from about 15 or 16, leaving the group when we reached 18. It was a revelation, meeting other queer teens. Every Friday was exciting and raucous. Lots of fun. Games, basic self defence, trips out to the seaside and country and once to Edinburgh, in a mini van and lots of gossiping and laughter. The people attending were from all walks of life, from council houses to large villas in Jesmond, but everyone supported each other. The group was facilitated by a gay youth worker, who worked for Newcastle Friend, a gay helpline. TGTG was a safe place, where we could experiment with who we were, try on different personalities, dress how we wanted, discover who we were and build on that. We were like a small alternative family. It was amazing.

I was lucky in that I already had a best friend to go along with. Someone I grew up with. We came out to each other when we were 13 years old. All these years later we are still best friends! Like family. He joined the group a little bit before me and persuaded me to go along. It was one of the best decisions I've ever made.

I still know one or two others from the group, though sadly, I discovered some have succumbed to AIDS.

I remember those days with much joy and happiness. We were all larger than life. We thought we knew it all, when in fact, we were just starting out with so far to go. It was a very special time and I loved it.[330]

In February 1983 the group was allowed to affiliate to the Newcastle Education Committee, thus enabling it to apply and receive grants. The decision to allow affiliation was taken by Newcastle's Youth, Community and Adult Education Committee. This decision was not without its critics. 'Rates cash for gay teenies' ran one headline in the *Newcastle Evening Chronicle*.[331] By 1986 the group was named the Tyneside Lesbian and Gay Youth Group. It was still receiving funding from Newcastle Council.[332]

On 23 September 1983 *Capital Gay* reported on GYM supporting the defence of PIE.

In 1983 the film *Framed Youth – the revenge of the teenage perverts* was completed. This film was produced by the Lesbian and Gay Youth Video Project. The film shows gay and lesbian young people interviewing passers-by on the streets of London about their views on homosexuality and lesbianism. The project involved a number of former members of the London Gay Teenage Group. Young lesbians and young gay men were the makers of the film. The main project members were Trill Burton, Pom Martin, Nicola Field, Rose Collis, Connie Giannaris, Toby Kettle, Jeff Cole and Jimmy Somerville. The film won the 1983 British Film Institute Grierson Award for Best Documentary. It was broadcast on Channel 4 in December 1986.[333]

During 1983 more information was emerging about AIDS and by the middle of the year there were at least 20 known cases in Britain. The first national conference on AIDS was organised the following year.[334] Although not exclusively affecting gay men, it was popularly portrayed as a 'gay plague'.

Lyn Thomas recalled:

I was treasurer until I left in 1986 – not quite sure what happened to
the bank account after that. Gill and Jon might know. I must admit
my archive was lost several moves ago ... LGYM (GYM until late
1984/early 1985) held a number of summer camps – first in Durham
over the August bank holiday weekend of the Durham GayFest
(1981), followed the next year with a week-long summer camp at
Fox Hagg Farm, near Sheffield, to coincide with the Sheffield Gay
Fest (1982). Then August Bank holiday week in Scarborough (1983),
then Capel Bangor near Aberystwyth (1984), and a final one as an
older friend of Lesbian & Gay Youth (I was 26) at Cummertrees, near
Annan (1985). The GYM calendar aimed to have a major meeting
(a weekend workshop) in London once or twice a year, a week-long
summer camp, and, in association with a local youth group, a weekend
workshop elsewhere. I attended ones in Southampton [possibly the
Southern Gay Youth Day held in Southampton March 1982], Stoke
on Trent, Edinburgh and Liverpool. The LGYM annual meeting was
usually held at summer camp. Plus there were committee meetings
open to all members held approximately monthly in London and
occasionally elsewhere, like Wolverhampton. Oh, Gay Fest grew
out of the Campaign for Homosexual Equality's AGM on August
Bank Holiday. They invited other organisations to meet and share
in an activist's weekend. Only two were held, Durham and Sheffield.
Sheffield was when CHE split into two organisation – The Gay
Community Organisation, which did social groups and support,
and CHE, the campaigning arm. Unfortunately that led rapidly to
the demise of CHE as the largest membership LGBT organisation
in the UK (or more properly England and Wales – Scotland and
Northern Ireland had their own organisations). The bank account
was necessary – we had Lesbian & Gay Youth to pay for, summer
camps and weekend workshop fees and a large membership (at one
point over 500 members).

The phone line, by the way, was a 'London Only' one in theory, and
that was paid for with a grant from the GLC. I was most impressed that
when we put in the application I was invited to County Hall and instead

of sitting in some reception room I went up to the office and met the official dealing with it at his desk, the epitome of open government.

Incidentally events like the summer camps would not have happened without the generous support of the London Gay Teenage Group – who hired the tents (10 six-person ones and two large marquees) from Sheffield onwards – from the Inner London Education Authority. The LGYM membership blossomed when the Agony Aunt in *Record Mirror*, Susanne Garrett, in reply to a lonely gay teen, said we had a penfriend scheme. In a week we had hundreds of letters. So we set one up and got them to join LGYM as the price of joining the scheme. It was truly impressive. Also the Aberystwyth camp took a detour to Wolverhampton to pick up me and supplies: rice, pasta, sacks of carrots, onions and potatoes etc. for most of the food at the summer camp.[335]

The London Gay Teenage Group AGM was held on 9 October 1983. The Constitution (passed at this AGM 1983) states that the Management Committee shall consist of:

4 members of the group elected by the group
4 other persons who are not members of the group and are 21 yrs +
A representative of ILEA is entitled to attend in advisory capacity
Others may be co-opted.
The Management Committee shall elect a Chairperson, Treasurer and
    Secretary.
The Committee shall meet no less than six times a year.
Group members may attend as non-voting participants.

At the end of the year the *Evening Standard* headline ran 'Rates cash for teenage gays'. The payment from the GLC to the LGTG was nothing new but this particular award of cash topped the £13,994 awarded the previous year (for 1983). 'The GLC is to hand out more than £20,000 of ratepayers' cash to a gay and lesbian group operating from a London Labour Party headquarters', reported Dick Murray. 'The Labour-controlled GLC's finance and general purposes committee agreed the payment... despite opposition from GLC Tory councillors'. Objection was based on the political association of the group, by being based at the Labour premises. This was in fact where the LGTG research project was based, in a basement but with no contact with the Labour Party above, not the actual LGTG, which was still based at Manor Gardens.[336] As Lorraine Trenchard explained in 2020, 'The office space (a basement room) was available and cheap/free? There was no political partisanship and we never had contact with those working above'.[337]

Chapter Eleven

SOMETHING TO TELL YOU, 1984

In February *Capital Gay* reported that 20 members of the LGTG went on a tin-rattling fundraising walk round various gay venues including The Quebec, Stallions, The London Apprentice and The Bell. A total of £49.05 was collected.[338]

Tom Midgley of the GYM wrote to Philip Conn of Friend in February 1984 pointing out that 400 people had joined GYM in the previous year, and 200 of these were to be part of the pen pal scheme. 'Our penfriend scheme, which started 9 months ago, has been our biggest success'.[339]

Something to tell you (1984) received wide distribution, largely thanks to the GLC. David Joad, LGTG chair, wrote the foreword. The book clearly spells out the experiences and needs of young lesbians and gay men in London at the time.

Much of the material in the book derives from the questionnaires completed. One thousand seven hundred questionnaires were distributed around London after a media campaign targeting young people under 21 who might consider themselves gay or lesbian. Four hundred and sixteen valid questionnaire returns were made. They came in mostly from males 18–20 years of age. One third of the returns were from women, again predominantly in the same age range. Thirty-two per cent of the respondents were still at school or college.

The book examined the experience of young people who identified as gay, lesbian or bisexual in the areas of school, family, work, college, relationships, 'coming out', pressures, problems and the police. The book contains numerous quotes from young people and tables charting things like who they had come out to, when they first had gay sex and such like. The appendixes included a brief summary of the history of the LGTG by Chris Heaume, a book list and useful contact addresses and numbers.

Eighty of the 416 returned valid questionnaires mentioned attempting suicide, reflecting 'the cumulative effects of a negative self image, problems at school, the experience of isolation, a lack of the usual support networks, family rejection and so on [which] can lead to a young person feeling quite helpless'.[340] Ken Livingstone referred to this finding and others in a debate in the House of Commons in December 1987 (see Chapter 13: 1987).

Ronnie Tumelty was also working as a youth worker at the group by the time the book was published. He was at the LGTG for nearly two years from the summer of 1983.

Josef Cabey recalled:

I first started going [to the LGTG] in 1984. I had previously attempted to come out first through daring to go to the only gay pub I knew of, The LA,[341] then trying a befriending group for men. Alas both of those experiences had my 17-year-old self running for the hills. Anyhow having plucked up the courage to go to LGTG I did that thing of walking up and down the road by Manor Gardens a million times before stepping onto the grounds. If I recall rightly I might have been met at the entrance by a member but not certain if I recall that correctly. OK so having made it through the door I must admit to first feeling a sense of shock and horror but also relief. Most people seemed so, so camp, which was scary for me at first. I remember someone was there in drag (later became one of the scene's drag troopers) that was so new to this Hackney boy. People appeared so loud and screechy and at first I could not locate anyone I thought I might get along with. I was basically quite introverted in nature and somewhat weighty. Certainly not the type everyone would likely come flocking to. It seemed like a big pink competition to out camp & bitch each other. However in actuality people were really nice on the whole and did welcome me, especially some of the guys on the committee and the youth workers. To cut a long story short I clearly was not scared off by any of it and attended solidly till sometime in 1985 and then on and off until I had got to that magic age of 21.

Have to say LGTG was one of the best things that ever happened to me. It certainly set me up on my young gay journey by introducing me to people my own age. I got to know lots of people there and managed to let my guard down somewhat. I loved our weekly visits to the Black Cap or La Cage and came to really enjoy the drag there. In fact on my first visit to the Cap with the group I bumped into an old school friend: something that produced a great deal of shock and awe for us both. I made some really good friends at the group (and even had one of those embarrassing and awkward moments by developing a crush on my closest mate lol!). I am still loosely in touch with a couple of people now all these years on. Naturally there are sad memories too as ex-members have passed on. I feel sadness when I recall one bright young guy, a really lovely person, and huddling with him in a corner gassing and giggling, like the kids we were, about a certain sexual activity he had experienced for the first time. It was mortifying when I found out he had later died of an AIDS-related illness.

As I said before I was quite introverted and sometimes felt intimidated by the discussion sessions that sometimes took place. I'm not sure that I contributed too much out of shyness. That is my recollection of it. My other recollection was of squirming every time a camera appeared and trying to disappear. Well that memory is certainly wrong, wrong, wrong as recently people have been posting photos from that time on an LGTG Facebook page and there I am quite a few times, not running, not squirming and actually looking pretty comfortable in the space and in some instances actually looking at the camera. Well I never![342]

Steve Lunniss:

I came to LGTG [September 1982] as a fairly unconfident young man trying to come to terms with my sexuality. In the next three years I changed immeasurably in confidence. I became a Chair of the group in Autumn 1984. As a result of this, I also became Vice Chair of London Union of Youth Clubs, a founder director of Streetwise, a committee member of London Lesbian and Gay Centre and had a career managing social care services.[343]

ILEA funding was only ever for the seconding of the youth workers to LGTG. They were effectively managed by the Chair and the MC [Management Committee]. The rent and phone and all other costs were paid for through tea money and fundraising: Jumble sales

– Holloway Road was great for the Irish community who loved a good jumble sale. I remember we often had problems with "shoplifters" who would drape a newspaper over their arm and scoop jumble into their bags. Tin shaking – we would go in the gay pubs...requiring us to receive the odd grope and dirty comment. Money was always tight and we were often slightly in arrears with rent. Martin [Collins] was great at keeping us on the straight and narrow, with up to date books.[344]

The Gay Youth Movement held a spring event at the University of London. The event included workshops, theatre shows and a disco but was marred by the theft of the £200 registration fees.[345]

The spring 1984 issue of *Gay Youth*, produced by the Gay Youth Movement, reported difficulties with two bookshops which previously stocked copies of *Gay Youth*. Bookplace in Peckham and Bread and Roses in Islington had issues with the magazine's support for paedophiles.[346] One reader wrote in to say she had been molested by an adult when she was six or seven, and although she supported most of what GYM stood for, she could not support PIE or paedophiles. There were surely many other young people who must have felt uneasy about the GYM stand on this issue. GYM was increasingly anti-everything and supporting every anti-establishment cause, not just PIE but also Sinn Féin, which at the time was silent on the IRA (Irish Republican Army). Later articles such as 'School is Shite' and 'Fuck Christmas' paint the tone.[347] GYM was beginning to make the GLF look very moderate by comparison. Some issues of *Gay Youth* contained inaccurate articles. For example that the South London Gay Young People's Group disaffiliated from GYM (after GYM accused it of being sexist), but this was untrue.[348] Perhaps because it was so extreme, GYM was by this time rather insignificant, and of no concern to the authorities. Little is written about it and apart from the copies of *Gay Youth* in the British Library and archives like Hall Carpenter, it has left little legacy. It did run a few summer camps, but it is disappointing that what could have been an excellent campaigning group was dominated by just a few angry young people who must have alienated most people they came into contact with.

Gay Youth issues have a marked absence of any practical safer sex information. Given the fact that at the time gay men were beginning to die of AIDS and that engaging in unprotected gay sex was like playing a game of Russian roulette, real help could have been provided for young people explaining measures they could take to protect themselves. How many gay men, young and old, were to become infected with this life-long illness because of the dearth of sound advice? Of course, some just ignored what dangers or advice there was. It was not until the end of 1986 that the government launched a massive public health campaign inclusive of gay men.

It was not just GYM that seemed to turn a blind eye to AIDS. The Essex Gay Youth Helpline news sheet in April 1984 stated 'Don't panic, AIDS is not as bad as it seems. At least, it is not any worse or more dangerous than many other so-called killer diseases'. After explaining correctly that it was not just a gay disease, the news sheet underplayed the seriousness of AIDS: 'Since AIDS "arrived" in this country, only 33–38 cases have been reported'.[349] Clearly it appears at this time many gay men did not see the serious dangers of having unprotected sex. Many people were quite unaware of the length of time it could take symptoms to appear and just how many carriers of HIV there were on the gay scene. The relaxed attitude seems very irresponsible, writing with hindsight. Clews (2017) documents the steady but slow progress in understanding the disease. It was not until 1985 that the extent to which gay people were getting infected became clearly evident and that gay men had to take this very seriously. The tone of a Gay Youth Helpline news sheet would be likely to be quite different by 1986.

The LGTG, being an organisation that lasted a lot longer than GYM, touched more lives. Members on average stayed about three to five months,[350] and the LGTG existed for well over 20 years. Attendance rates fluctuated but were usually anything between 15–40. It can be estimated that well over 2,000 young people attended the LGTG over the 25 years, 1976–2000, and that is not counting people who just popped in to the group for one or two sessions.[351]

The first national young lesbian summer camp was held at Ingleton in Yorkshire from 3–7 September. Lorraine Trenchard helped to organise this event and the work she did went towards her Youth Service training course assessment. Thirty-five women, including youth workers, attended. As well as the Young Lesbian Group (North London), a group from Sheffield and the South London Young Lesbian Group were also there.[352]

In June 1984 the *Times Educational Supplement* ran an article on 'Young and gay'. The article spoke of the lack of any support in schools for gay youngsters. The only authority which had made any provision was ILEA, which in 1979 recognised the London Gay Teenage Group and had given them a grant each year since. In 1983–84 this amounted to £6,223, of which £5,765 was salary for two part-time youth workers. GYM organiser Graham Pyper,[353] aged 26, is quoted as saying, 'We demand equality with heterosexual people'. The article also quotes, 'Fifteen-year-old Barry, as he asks to be called, points out how his education suffered by his "assertive homosexuality and refusal to conform at school". Barry says a teacher called him a poof and he visits the Child Guidance Clinic and is confronted with child psychologists and education therapists'. The article says it is difficult to assess the group's influence with any accuracy. The DES (Department of Education and Science) had not heard of them. 'Their aggressively political stance and the strongly implied support for the Paedophile Information Exchange in *Gay Youth* is hardly calculated to win support for their central aims or to endear them to the general public', wrote Hugh David. David also spoke to 18-year-old Danny, who dismissed GYM as jerks. He said he had been to a couple of meetings but found gay politics so boring. He said he was in the 4th Year (Year 10 in modern schools) when he started going to Heaven (gay disco).[354]

GYM were running a penfriend scheme for under-26-year-olds. The following are examples of some of the adverts they ran:

Phil, Box J22, male 17 Feltham, Middlesex. Like pop music, computers, and going to the pictures and concerts. I'll write to anyone who wants to correspond with me, preferably same age or older.

Caroline, Box B23, female 18 Lincoln. I like music (e.g. Siouxsie and the Banshees, Xmal, PIL, Virgin Prunes and Divine), going to gigs and nightclubs. I love food, esp. eating out. & travelling to larger cities, mainly for clothes, clubs and meeting new people. I dislike arrogant and narrow-minded people, obsessive drinking and smoking. I'd like someone to write, genuine and sincere, and who agrees with my views.

Not everyone was happy with the penfriend scheme. An 18-year-old from Hertfordshire wrote to the LGTG, complaining not just about the extreme left-wing politics of LGYM but also the befriending scheme. His letter survived amongst papers kept by Steve Lunniss:

Dear Steven,

I am a member of the LGYM and I am totally pissed off with it, they always claim what great facilities they provide etc. They have done nothing for me! This morning they sent me a 'contact list' of gay teenagers in my area. This area consisted of about 20 people living in

Bucks, Berks, Herts, Beds and Northants – very local I must admit. The nearest person my age (I am 18) lives over 30 miles away. Most of them are well over 21, which is hardly youth.

All the stuff they send out consists mainly of left wing propaganda. They seem to be a bunch of egotistical bastards who see LGYM to be an extension of Militant Tendency.

Isn't homosexuality about relationships and support for each other?

I intend to get rid of all links with LGYM asap and I would be really grateful if you could send me details of your organisation as from what I can see LGTG seems to be 100X better.[355]

At Pride in 1984 the LGTG had three placards with the contact telephone number shown in large numbers. In addition, the Gay Youth Movement had a banner. Some photos of both banners in use at Pride events can be found in the Bishopsgate archives.[356]

The 'Change to Change' NAYC Conference was held in Nottingham 6–8 July 1984. Graham Yelland, Steven Lunniss, David Joad, Adam Threadgold and Jamie Styles attended from the LGTG. Steve Lunniss recalled in 2020: 'We received a great deal of harassment and homophobic jibes, so we approached the organisers and asked to speak to conference. David Joad made a very powerful speech which others of us joined in. We received a standing ovation at the end and many apologies and positive comments later.'[357]

After retiring as chair of the LGTG, David Joad was asked to sit on the British Youth Council from 1984 to 1985, primarily because of his role in LGTG. He was vice-chair of the UK Organising Committee of International Youth Year (1985).

On 31 July 1984 the GLC issued a press release, 'GLC abolition threatens gay research'.[358] The gay research referred to included that work of Lorraine Trenchard and Hugh Warren, who that year published *Talking about Young Lesbians* (1984) and *Talking about School* (1984), to complement *Something to tell you* (1984). *Talking about Youth Work* (1985) came the following year. *Talking about Young Lesbians* was aimed at young women questioning their sexuality and was largely composed of young lesbians talking about their experiences. The booklet included a number of case studies, a collection of cartoons and photographs, and a list of contacts (Lesbian Line phone numbers and details of the Young Lesbian Group, LGTG, South London Gay Young People's Group and South London Young Lesbian Group).

On 7 October the LGTG held its AGM at Manor Gardens.

Towards the end of summer 1984 GYM activity had come to a temporary halt.

On 10 November 1984 a demo was held in Rugby after the council there refused to employ any gay or lesbian people. The GYM banner was broken in scuffles with the police. Eighteen people were arrested. Chris Smith MP addressed the demo and announced himself as gay. He was the first 'out' gay MP.[359, 360]

Lyn Thomas issued a notice in November 1984 announcing that an emergency general meeting would be held on 15–16 December at the Birmingham Lesbian and Gay Centre, 291 Corporation Street. The notice stated, 'During the months of Aug, Sept and Oct, GYM has had problems. To put it simply, GYM came to a grinding halt! The new people running GYM were handed over things in a very good order. However they had failed to turn up at a meeting in November and now members were demanding work be done to keep GYM going'.[361]

By January 1985 the title of *Gay Youth* had changed to the *Lesbian and Gay Youth* magazine and GYM had become the Lesbian and Gay Youth Movement.

Chapter Twelve

HIV AND AIDS EDUCATION, 1985

In 1985 the LGTG was renamed the LLGTG (London Lesbian and Gay Teenage Group). This reflected the fact that more women had started coming to the group.[362]

A duplicated publication called *Visions* started appearing in 1985. It was subtitled 'the magazine of the LGTG'[363]. The December edition was on green paper. It features Jamie Styles, aged 19, describing how he moved 300 miles to get work and was then sacked. His boss told the DHSS that Jamie had left of his own accord, but Jamie reported he suffered abuse because he was open about being gay and that his boss had sacked him because he was openly gay. 'Fortunately, I have gay friends who were supportive and helpful. As a result, it proved to be not too damaging for me. One thing I often wonder about is how such an experience would affect someone who does not have the support that a gay youth group provides', Jamie commented. *Visions* was stocked in Gay's the Word and Housman's bookshops. It was printed at the Islington Bus Company.[364]

The Spring Festival of GYM was held over the weekend 4–6 May.

Kim Nagle started as a part-time youth worker at the LGTG on 5 May 1985. She had replaced Ronnie Tumelty, whose last shift was 24 March 1985.[365] Another youth worker at the group then was Mark Walder.

In June 1985, Chris Heaume, who was then working at the Islington Green Youth Centre, wrote in the Islington Area Youth Office newsletter about how 'gay young people might be encouraged to question the present situation in which they find themselves and the kind of support they need to be able to respond in a positive way'. He went on to point out that, 'still the majority of lesbian and gay young people live in fear and ignorance of opportunities.'[366]

Anthony Hillin, an Australian working as a social worker in London, took the post vacated by Gregg Blachford (who left in July 1985). Anthony, who had done work with the Terrence Higgins Trust, had recently been appointed as the first coordinator of PACE (Project for Advice, Counselling and Education) at the new London Lesbian and Gay Centre in Cowcross Street. The PACE position was full-time and LGTG was seven hours a week. In 2020 he recalled:

I was pleased to be a part of the LGTG not least because it was a rare example of a group run by and for young people. Many initiatives held this as an aspiration but few fully achieved it. From my social work training I was familiar with concepts of Community Development and self-determination, of assisting communities to come together and find common cause, and to organise to meet those needs. This approach built capacity for individuals to create change, whereas working with individuals separately did nothing to bridge isolation and risked creating dependency, a feeling that we need to rely on someone else to make a difference or to heal us, rather than developing a sense of belief in our own ability to create change.

During my job interview I had spoken passionately about the urgent need for effective HIV prevention and of the complexities of undertaking this with teenagers, given their developmental needs and vulnerabilities. I explained that I believed a holistic approach was needed, which located sexual health within a wider well-being program that addressed self-esteem and internalised oppression, which developed the social skills and confidence necessary to negotiate safer sex and that addressed other aspects of self-care including nutrition and drug and alcohol issues. I had highlighted the need for social connection and psychological strategies to cope with challenges such as managing stress and anxiety. I stressed that this shouldn't be imposed on the group but would need to evolve with members actively involved in the design, delivery and ownership. After the interview I wondered if I'd been too intense but I had felt they needed to know what they'd be getting if I was appointed. I was relieved to be told by Steve Lunniss, Chair, and the management group that I was chosen because they also thought it was vital to address HIV prevention and the other issues I'd laid out at interview.[367]

After settling in at the group Anthony Hillin observed how things were working at the group:

I could see many other things were working really well. I was moved by the sense of camaraderie and enjoyment members felt in each other's company. The administration of the group was running smoothly, and the structure was well thought through. This was in no small part due to the impressive efficiency of the chair, Steve Lunniss, and behind-the-scenes, the commitment and skills of the Management Committee and my predecessor as youth worker, Gregg Blachford. All seemed to have a good understanding of the range of challenges and issues faced by same sex attracted young people. Trenchard and Warren's (1984) research had helped to confirm and quantify these issues.

Those early visits did raise some concerns for me, however. I noticed variation in the way the group responded to new members. Those who were more attractive often received more attention and seemed to become integrated into friendship networks more readily. Sometimes this appeared to be related to physical attractiveness but also due to personality and social skills. This isn't surprising. It can happen in any group regardless of age and is perhaps to be expected more among young people, who may still be developing their social skills and identity. To the group's great credit, an attempt was made to welcome all new people. I could see how these attempts at inclusion fell away with new people who were shy or awkward. There didn't seem to be a lack of awareness that welcoming new people was important but more a lack of confidence about how to do this when it didn't flow easily. Apart from the youth workers talking with new members, sometimes it seemed this welcoming was being performed as a duty by just a few more conscientious members. I was acutely aware that there was a lot of hope and sometimes desperation behind new members reaching out to the group and turning up for the first time. It wasn't hard to imagine the negative impact on them if they didn't feel welcomed and accepted here, of all places, among their own kind, after the likely isolation and possible rejection in other parts of their lives.[368]

In 1985 ILEA set up their 'Relationships and Sexuality Project'. In 1986 2,000 copies of *Materiography* no 11 (ILEA 1986) were produced, a guide to resources and materials. Then three videos were produced as teaching aides (Harris, 1990).

David Joad, Jamie Styles and Steve Lunniss from the LGTG, attended the

International Gay Youth Congress in July. Ireland's National Gay Federation hosted this in Dublin. At this conference, the Congress called upon the World Health Organization to remove homosexuality from its list of mental illnesses, and UK education authorities to remove minimum age limits from the conditions of registration and funding for gay youth groups.

Jayson Mannings recalled in 2020:

> I discovered the Gay Teenage Group, as I believe it was known at the time, back in 1985. I worked in a summer project at Manor Gardens working with young people with differing disabilities and their siblings.
>
> I was 15 at the time and was faced with lots of homophobic abuse at school, both from the students and passively from some of the teaching staff. A lot of my teachers were fearful of confronting issues due to some of the backlash of HIV/Aids in the press.
>
> I remember at the time you had to be 16 to join the group and there was a lot of discussion about if I could join or not, but to be honest I look back now and wonder if I would have survived without it.
>
> The group was a safe space for me to grow, somewhere that was safe and I didn't feel I had to be something other than myself.
>
> One of the most important things I think I took away from the group was to be able to know that being gay was not wrong and that I wasn't a freak and it was all right to be gay. I became the proud gay man that I still am today. I made some amazing friends who supported me through some very dark times. I even got a penfriend who, through the group page, I have been able to reconnect with. I'm not sure she realised how much I valued her support and friendship at the time.
>
> I remember attending my first pride with the group and how safe I felt with everyone there looking out for me. When I was 16 I met my first real boyfriend, Roy. He was a little older and it was love at first sight. We were together until we were both 20 and are still in contact today. I just wonder if we would have been together longer if gay marriage was legal back then.[369]

The penfriend mentioned by Jayson probably came through the LGTG revised penfriend scheme launched in the summer of 1985. By January 1986 it had 31 people signed up to it, of which just three were female. A report on the scheme contained a breakdown of the ages of the 31 in the scheme:

- under 16 – 3
- age 16 – 6
- age 17 – 9
- age 18 – 5
- age 19 – 6
- age 20 – 2

Nine of the 31 were attenders at the group. Others lived as far away as Devon, the West Midlands and even one in the Orkney Islands. The aim of the scheme was 'to attempt to combat some of the isolation that young lesbians, gay men and bisexuals feel when they do not know anyone in the area in which they live who feels like they do'.[370]

The GLC issued their Lesbian and Gay Charter in a declaration 'Changing the World'. Copies of the LGTG publication *Something to tell you* were sent out with the declaration to hundreds of organisations. The GLC-funded London Lesbian and Gay Centre had opened in December 1984.[371] The GLC also gave a grant of £32,000 to the Stonewall Housing Association.[372]

In 1985 the East London and Essex Gay Youth Helpline were running weekly discos called 'The Alternatre' on Wednesdays in the Euston Tavern, London to raise money to support their work.[373] The helpline at that time had been running for two years, providing a service for under-26-year-olds. It was run from Steve Power's flat in Barking and Martin Collins and Simon Basler were involved.[374] They wrote to all the Essex and East London Members of Parliament concerning the age of consent. Two youth groups were set up for Essex and East London. The Mid-Essex Gay Youth Group (under 26) met in Chelmsford. The Young Gay Women and Men group (under 26) met at the King George IV pub in Ida Street, Poplar, London E14.[375]

Chapter Thirteen

ABOLITION OF THE GREATER LONDON COUNCIL.
GOVERNMENT AIDS CAMPAIGN. THE 'LOONY LEFT',
1986-87

The mid-1980s were when many of the advances in gay and lesbian recognition and provision started to be pushed back. The activities of some Labour councils in London, the Greater London Council (GLC) and ILEA sparked a reaction from those who felt things had gone too far. Politicians in both of the two major political parties began to realise what an important part of electoral success or failure support for lesbian and gay policies might play. That is, more votes would be lost than won by supporting gay rights!

Meanwhile the 10th anniversary of the LGTG was marked by a party held on Tuesday 18 February 1986 at the LLGC. By this time the group had reverted to its original name. As Anthony Hillin recalled: 'The number of women attending the LGTG was small and there were considerable periods when there were none. The group eventually came to the view that having "lesbian" in the title was false advertising and this concern outweighed the original intention of indicating a welcome to young women, hence the name was changed back'.[376]

LGTG had success with a documentary video film called *Democracy*, made in 1986, which won third prize in the David Harlech Democracy Award. Sixty groups had competed for the award (age limit for groups was 25). Michael Johnson was director of the film. The winning certificate lists three people: Mari Peacock, Mike Sage, Julian Withers. HTV West asked those involved down to Bristol to re-record it for Channel 4. Excerpts of the video were broadcast on 6 October 1986 on Channel 4 (*Democracy Rules OK?*).[377]

LGYM and the LGTG were in open conflict by 1986.[378] GYM published part of a letter purporting to be from the LGTG to Ken Livingstone at County Hall talking of the internal divisions within the LGYM and its failure to provide effective support for young people, and suggesting that the organisation was in a state of near collapse. GYM responded by saying the LGTG was controlled by adults, unlike the LGYM. This was a bit ironic given that LGYM was mostly run by young adults and the LGTG was run by under-21-year-olds!

Martin Collins recalled some of his activities with the LGYM:

LGYM had a phone line in Woolwich, London… It was pretty much run by London members. There was a monthly fund-raising disco at the LL&GC called the Crèche Club, DJ'd by David L. When we passed 26 birthdays, I think the organisation died…[379]

I was in love with Adam T, who remained a good friend after a brief affair. Adam became a leisure assistant at Southwark swimming pools: I picked up on his excellent front and back stroke in the pool. Scarborough [1983] was my first [summer camp], there was a circus in the adjoining field I think … Amazing how ten six-person tents and 12–14 passengers were packed into an ILEA minibus driven certainly on one or possibly both Aberystwyth & Cummertrees, Annan summer camps. Even more amazing that the minibus got up some hills. Certainly one year we were loading outside 'Wee Nooke' [home of Jon Pyper in Caledonian Road, King's Cross].

I remember driving a minibus from Hackney Community Transport to a Southampton weekend workshop. When everyone had been dropped back late Sunday night at Manor Gardens LGTG, my last passenger, was a mixed race black guy who had his hands all over me on the journey back to London whilst I was driving.[380]

Jon Pyper (then known as Graham Pyper) went to the Sheffield camp (1982), the GYM Day event (GYM'LL Fix It) and was involved in the LGYM up until about 1986. Jon recalled:

It was a group not just interested in gay issues, but also in youth issues. Jay McLaren, Tom Midgley, Keith Trotman and Jeff Vernon were powerful proponents of the rights of youth, and advocates for those without a voice, those who are disenfranchised. They stand up not only to the abuse suffered by people because they are gay, but also because they are young. I will speak only for myself here. Abused youths do not have pretty voices. Damaged youths do not have nice ideas. Traumatised youths do not care for niceties. Neglected youths do not become the poster boys of politics ... The magazine [*Gay Youth*] is clearly about young, abused, lesbians and gays discovering their voices, developing their ideas, finding their place in the world and needing the absolute right to scream from the rooftops 'fuck the lot of you'. Does this have credibility? Depends on how you choose to look at it. The fact that both LGTG and LGYM were desperately needed is a sad, sorry indictment of society. The fact that they did exist, and achieved all that they did is to be applauded. They helped victims to recover, and saved lives. Please don't ever forget that.[381]

It is not difficult to understand the anger, but the politics of GYM have led to it becoming little more than a footnote in history when it could have been so much more. The author attended the NUS Gay Rights Conference in Leeds in the winter of 1979–80, and a similarly narrow blanket idealist approach was expressed in that movement. He recalls, one of the main movers in the organisation was basically saying that a Marxist revolution would solve everything and liberate us all:

At which point I stood up and challenged that view. He said 'I had put the cat among the pigeons!' Marxist liberation and gay rights!! These people were blind to history. I see the same problems with the hard left today. Basically alienating debate and lambasting anyone with an alternative view.[382]

In Ealing, the Council's Lesbian and Gay Rights Working Party recommended that posters advertising the helplines Gay Switchboard and Lesbian Line be put up in secondary schools. This led the local MP Harry Greenway to contact the Education Secretary, Kenneth Baker, asking him to stop this from happening.[383]

By the time of the LGTG AGM, on 9 October 1986, the number of women attending the LGTG had fallen back. It was believed that a lot of sexism in the group still discouraged women.[384] From Friday 31 October to Sunday 2 November 1986 Birmingham Lesbian and Gay Centre, at 291 Corporation Street, hosted a Lesbian and Gay Youth Festival for under-26-year-olds.[385]

At the end of the year it was estimated that there were about 30,000 HIV-infected people in the UK, three-quarters of them in London. At the rate the infection was spreading it was estimated that there would be 200,000 people infected in the UK by 1988, with 15–30% of them developing AIDS.[386] By August 1986 Norman Fowler wanted to step up the public education campaign. He proposed that an AIDS leaflet be delivered to every household in the UK.[387] In November 1986 the British government finally grasped the scale of the AIDS problem, setting up a cabinet committee devoted to combatting what was rapidly becoming an epidemic. Twenty million pounds was earmarked for a publicity campaign, £5 million of which was to be spent on television commercials which could be adapted for cinema. Early in the following year a massive health education campaign about HIV and AIDS was delivered ('AIDS: Don't Die of Ignorance').[388] Over 23 million households were leafleted. The campaign stressed that it was a deadly disease and promoted help and advice. Most gay men took precautions, but many had already contracted HIV and many died of AIDS. Sadly a number of those who had attended the LGTG were victims of this disease. Deaths from AIDS peaked in the UK in 1994–95 and, although declining since, in 2018 there were 473 deaths among people living with HIV.[389]

GAY AND LESBIAN CHILDREN UNDER 16

When the LGTG was formally recognised as an officially registered youth group, ILEA stipulated that the group could only cater to those aged 16 to 21 years old. Jane Dixon, who was appointed by ILEA as a specialist youth officer for work with gay and lesbian young people in 1985, raised the issue of provision for lesbian and gay young people under 16. In March 1986 Dixon set up an ILEA Lesbian and Gay Youth Groups under-16s working party. Meetings were held at the LLGC in April.[390]

The issue of under-16-year-olds attending the LGTG had caused Islington Area Youth Office some concern, as the grant of official status by ILEA was dependant on adhering to the age rules of group members being over 16 but under 21. At a meeting of the Area Youth Committee in May 1986 it was noted that the lower age limit of 16 was an ILEA policy. Minutes of the meeting record that 'Opinion on this issue was divided, but overall it was felt that the age limit of sixteen should be abandoned. A worker from the Lesbian and Gay Teenage Group would be invited when the topic would next be discussed'.[391] Subsequently, Islington Youth Office prepared a paper arguing for the establishment of a statutory detached youth service for unattached gay and lesbian young people in

Islington. One reason for establishing this provision was to cater to the needs of under-16-year-olds, who were excluded from the LGTG and the Young Lesbian Project. The provision would require one male and one female worker and premises. It was proposed to work jointly with Camden and that each authority provide one post each. By establishing this project the LGTG would then have a service that they could refer under-16-year-olds to.[392]

Meanwhile, in July members of the South London Lesbian and Gay Young People's Group (based in Catford) wrote to ILEA calling for the lower age restriction to be amended. The 12 signatories to the letter all stated that they 'knew of their sexuality before the age of sixteen'.[393] Some members of the LGTG also wrote to ILEA arguing that the minimum age for attendance at lesbian and gay youth groups should be dropped.[394] In October 1986 Dixon wrote a 10-page report, 'Working with young lesbians and young gay men in the youth service'.[395] This report became public early in 1987.

1987

Dixon's report came to public notice in March 1987. The report outlines how the existing young lesbian and gay groups have been operating in London and the 'positive work in these groups starts from the basis that there is nothing intrinsically wrong with being lesbian and gay'. Twelve such groups are mentioned:

Lewisham Young Gay Men's Group[396]
Lewisham Young Lesbian Group
Lambeth Young Lesbian Group
London Gay Teenage Group (Islington)
Young Lesbian Group (Islington)
Hackney Young Lesbian Group
Hammersmith and Fulham Young Lesbian Group
Notting Hill Gay Young Men's Group (Kensington and Chelsea)
Notting Hill Young Lesbian Group
Tower Hamlets Gay Young Men's Group
Wandsworth Young Lesbian Group
Wandsworth Gay Young Men's Group

In addition, Dixon notes that 'in Westminster 1,000 part-time hours are allocated to lesbian and gay youth work, with the use of the centre in Trafalgar Square as a base and venue'.

On page four of the report Dixon outlines why the ruling on a lower age limit of 16 for the LGTG (at the time it was first registered) 'is contradictory and discriminatory'. Other youth provision (heterosexuality assumed) includes 12- to 15-year-olds. The needs of under-16-year-old lesbians and gays were not being met. On page six Dixon states that 'Continuing lack of provision for this age range (12–16) has implications for the mental health and welfare of these young people'. The paper points out that gay and lesbian young people under 16 do not feel welcome or included in mainstream youth provision.

The report went to the London Youth Committee. Her Majesty's Inspector (Department of Education and Science) John Broadbent, read the report and commented on it being very interesting and informative, and asked for a meeting with Dixon to discuss the issues raised.[397] Some of the tabloid newspapers also read the report and were commenting on it. The *Daily Mail* reported 'Gay clubs report angers Morrell' and went on to say:

A militant feminist's call to allow children as young as 12 into gay clubs has been attacked by her own Labour authority chief.

Mrs Frances Morrell, leader of ILEA, said yesterday she was 'outraged'. And she added: 'I apologise to parents for any anxiety this story might have caused'.

She hastily summonsed officials to top-level meetings after the report by Miss Jane Dixon, the authority's specialist youth officer for homosexuals was leaked to the *Daily Mail*.[398]

The issue of promoting provision for 12- to 15-year-old gay and lesbian youngsters was also taken up by *The Star*. Under the headline 'No age limit on filth' the report called Jane Dixon:

… a disturbingly dotty woman … wants children of 12 to be allowed to join lesbian and gay clubs. Ms Dixon says that: 'Refusing them admission is heterosexist and breaches the ILEA Equal Opportunities Code'. Ms Dixon is self-evidently mad, and her proposal utterly sickening.[399]

Shortly before the story about Jane Dixon's proposals emerged, Labour lost the Greenwich by-election on 26 February 1987. The far-left candidate,

Deirdre Wood, was torn apart by certain sections of the media. The SDP (Social Democratic Party)/Liberal Alliance won the seat. Following this, Patricia Hewitt wrote a letter to Frank Dobson (Labour MP) which was leaked to the newspapers. Hewitt at the time was press secretary to Neil Kinnock (leader of the Labour Party). The letter referred to the left-wing London councils (in particular Islington) and their policies, such as supporting lesbian and gay rights of children aged 12 years old and running courses in heterosexualism. These Labour councils were becoming known to be dominated by 'the loony left'. 'The Loony Left' headlines appeared in March 1987.[400] Hewitt was worried about the effect this would have on Labour's election chances:

> It is obvious from our own polling, as well as from the doorstep, that the 'London effect' is now very noticeable. The 'Loony Labour Left' is now taking its toll; the gays and lesbians issue is costing us dear amongst the pensioners and fear of extremism and higher taxes/rates is particularly prominent in the GLC area.[401]

Patricia Hewitt's fears were confirmed by the results in the 1987 general election, held on 11 June, when Margaret Thatcher's Conservative government were returned with a majority of 147 seats over Labour. Thatcher became the first leader to win three general elections in a row since 1820, when the Earl of Liverpool achieved this with, of course, a much smaller electorate.

One of the billboard posters used by the Conservatives in the general election was headed up: 'Is this Labour's idea of a comprehensive education?' Under the heading there were three books. The first one had the slogan 'Young gay & proud' on the cover. The final one had 'The play book for kids about sex'. As Weeks (2016) remarked: the government that followed had a 'new emphasis on social and moral issues'.[402]

The last known issue of the *Lesbian and Gay Youth* magazine (issue 21, summer 1987) stated the summer camp would be in either the Lake District or the New Forest. The previous year's camp was advertised (spring 1986, issue 18) as being in North Devon, 2–10 August 1986.[403] The LGYM 1987 summer camp in the Lake District was documented in photos and an account by Russell Christie which is deposited in the Bishopsgate Institute archives.[404] Russell Christie, aged 22, was living in Nottingham at the time. Russell's notes state that Jeff Vernon was the main facilitator of the trip. The photos he has deposited with the Bishopsgate are well annotated with details of many of the young people on the trip (about 15 in all, just two of them women). Russell recalled:

We kissed each other openly in the fields and in the streets. The week was spent mostly swimming, climbing, walking, talking and sitting round the fire. A ten-year-old boy tagged along: Elton, the adopted orphan waif from London.

The LGYM was still going in December 1987 but sometime after that it seems to have folded.

The International Lesbian and Gay Youth Organisation (ILGYO) held its 4th Annual Conference in London, 2–9 August 1987, at Imperial College. A reception for the conference was held in Islington Town Hall on 3 August hosted by Councillor Bob Crossman.[405] Previous conferences had been held in 1984 (Amsterdam), 1985 (Dublin, where the IGYIP International Gay Youth Information Pool was established) and 1986 (Oslo).[406] The London conference programme came with a word of advice: 'Britain sadly is not yet as sexually liberated as many other countries' and warning delegates about the danger of kissing or showing affection in public, and that sexual acts between men were still illegal if either or both party were under 21.

The programme papers list gay youth organisations throughout Europe, including the LGTG in Manor Gardens, The North London Young Lesbian Group (Manor Gardens), Gay Young London Group,[407] Young Black Lesbian Group in Peckham,[408] Sunderland Gay Youth Group, Bristol Lesbian and Gay Youth Group, and the NUS Lesbian and Gay Caucus.[409] [410] At the end of the conference a mass 'kiss in' was performed in Piccadilly Circus to protest against treatment meted out to gay people when they kiss publicly.[411]

An ILEA video (Learning Resources Branch) called A Different Story: First Feelings was produced in 1987 as part of the Relationships and Sexuality Project. It was made for use in schools and starred Brian Healey, Ayo Oyebade, Fred Vogelius, Anna Tan, Davina Cooper, Barbara, Keith and Ritu Khurana. Lorraine Trenchard and Hugh Warren were the researchers for the production and Paul Patrick and Liz Dibb were the educational advisors.[412]

Concerns about the content and availability of the novel The Milkman's on His Way by David Rees (Gay Men's Press 1982) were raised with the Prime Minister's office in March 1987, influencing subsequent support for section 28. It was pointed out that the book, which contained graphic gay sex descriptions, was included in ILEA's Positive Resources booklet and recommended for young people aged 15-plus. A 15-year-old girl had managed to get a copy in the children's section of Harringay Library. The book is the story of a boy called Ewan and his gay sexual awakening.[413]

Jane Dixon's proposals, for provision for gay and lesbian young people aged under 16, were clearly radical for the time. They came to fruition in the radical boroughs of Islington and Camden. The North London Line (NLL) was a statutory group for young gay people, run by Islington Council, established to include support for young gay or lesbian people in the London boroughs of Islington and Camden. Set up in September 1987, it was jointly funded by both boroughs and provided for detached youth work. Jane Dixon and Ray Walker created the organisation and appointed Maureen Hand and Brian Healey as its first paid youth workers. Maureen, who attended the LGTG 1979–80, did a three-year youth work course at the YMCA National College in Walthamstow prior to her job at NLL. The first few meetings of the NLL were at Manor Gardens and then they moved to Highbury.

And by 1988 under-16-year-olds were certainly attending the LGTG. As James Byrne (chairperson, 1987–88) recalled:

As for allowing those under 16 to attend, we certainly did have members below the age of 16. I can't tell you if this was officially approved of or if we just turned a blind eye. I can remember several people under the age of 16 and I even remember one boy being brought to us by his parents who wanted to first check out the environment before entrusting him to us.[414]

The group took some risk by allowing under-16-year-olds in at this time. As Anthony Hillin points out it was a 'don't ask, don't tell' approach:

The group was concerned about the support needs of same sex attracted young people under 16 years of age and had lobbied for service provision for this population. Given the lack of provision, inevitably some under-16s contacted the group. The groups age range was explained to all contacts and a don't ask, don't tell approach prevailed. Under-16s quickly picked up on this and were adept at presenting an acceptable self. Most were all too experienced in keeping some personal things private and quickly grasped the nuances of this approach.[415]

Meanwhile, Anthony Hillin was continuing his valuable supportive work at the LGTG, including some residential weekends for the group. Matthew Scudamore recalled one weekend the group had at Bore Place, Kent:

This was run by Anthony Hillin and a woman whose name I cannot recall. I remember a Chinese boy relating his story and everyone was in tears. A fashion show was improvised with Michael Johnson doing the commentary as people came down a wooden staircase.[416]

As Anthony Hillin recalled in 2020:

The venue was Bore Place in Kent. I'd visited it previously and knew it would be appropriate. Despite the name, the weekend was anything but boring. Members showed rapt attention to each other's stories. There were heart-rending disclosures and moving accounts of surviving abuse and rejection. Opportunities for serious discussion were interspersed with time to celebrate positives and to have fun. We demonstrated that it didn't need to be either/or, heavy or light, that it was possible to move between different emotional states and outlooks and this could be an important part of self-care.

Twenty members attended. The ILEA provided a minibus. The group subsidised the cost to members. Those who could afford to make a financial contribution were invited to and those who could not were still welcome.

Some members had never spent time in the countryside and were amazed to see cows up close or were surprised by the night-time sounds, silence and darkness away from the city buzz and glow.[417]

On 15 December 1987 the House of Commons was debating the 'Prohibition on promoting homosexuality by teaching or by publishing material'.

The following are extracts of the record of the debate published in Hansard. Chris Smith spoke of the proposed legislation:

The second motive is a desire to change the climate so that to be gay or lesbian is to feel and to be treated as a second-class citizen. The climate has changed. There is more intolerance now than there was five or 10 years ago. The House cannot have failed to notice that last Saturday there was an arson attack on the offices of the *Capital Gay* newspaper, or that, during that same—[Interruption.]

Tony Banks (MP Newham North West) then remarked:

On a point of order, Mr. Speaker. I heard the hon. Member for Lancaster

[Mrs. Kellett-Bowman] say that it was quite right that *Capital Gay* should have been fire—

Mr Speaker:

Order. That is not a point of order. [Interruption.] Order. Hon. Members should not behave in the House like that. [Interruption.] Order. I heard nothing— [Interruption.] Order. Was it unparliamentary?

Mrs Kellett-Bowman:

I am quite prepared to affirm that it is quite right that there should be an intolerance of evil.

Ken Livingstone in that debate spoke about the LGTG survey work which the GLC sponsored:

I also wish to deal with the reality of life for lesbians and gay men and to base it upon a survey that was the subject of massive attack by many Conservative Members. That survey was the result of a grant given to the Gay Teenage Group by the GLC to examine the problems of gay teenagers in London. That group conducted a major, in-depth survey of over 400 young homosexuals between the ages of 15 and 21. Its conclusions were published, but disappeared in the wave of other press interest in the aftermath of the election in 1983 [The report was actually published in 1984 but Livingstone may have seen the findings earlier]. Its conclusions were horrifying. It was not propaganda, but the result of scientific analysis of what happens to young lesbians and gay men living in the city.

That survey showed that three out of five had been verbally abused, that one in five had been beaten up, that one in 12 had been sent to a psychiatrist, that one in 10 had been thrown out of their homes because of their sexuality and that one in 10 had been sent to a doctor in the hope that the doctor would cure them. However, the most horrifying statistic was that one in five of those young lesbians and gay men had attempted to commit suicide because of the anguish, loneliness and despair that they felt.

All Conservative Members must ask themselves whether the Bill will increase that despair, or reduce it… Society is not geared to help someone aged 13 or 14 who realises that he or she is gay or lesbian. Whom do they turn to for advice? The survey conducted by the Gay Teenage Group showed that 42 per cent of children who turned to their parents were rejected, were told that they were suffering from some sort of disease and were virtually excluded from the family. Parents are unable to cope with that situation.

The survey revealed that at school 25 per cent of young homosexuals felt isolated, that 21 per cent suffered verbal abuse, that 12 per cent were beaten up and that 7 per cent felt ostracised. How will the amendment tackle that?

…I shall take one quotation from the study by the Gay Teenage Group, which shows what the problem is for a young man who discovers that he is gay: 'I remember an incident in the third year when some lad asked me if I was queer. I denied it of course and I immediately withdrew into my shell even further. I tried suicide with a bottle of pills a couple of nights later. It didn't work of course. It just made me ill for about a week. Nobody realised what I'd done and I didn't tell them'. That is the reality that we face.[418]

The comment by Elaine Kellett-Bowman, Member of Parliament for Lancaster, is often quoted as one of the most anti-gay comments made in public by a prominent person at the time.

The LGYM advertised a festival on Saturday and Sunday 20–21 December 1987 with a disco on the Friday night before. It is not known if the event went ahead, but the author has found no trace of the LGYM after that.

Chapter Fourteen

SECTION 28 AND PRETENDED FAMILIES, 1988

On January 9 1988 there was a 'Stop clause 27' (became clause 28 and then section 28) march in London. The London Gay Teenage Group were there. The *Pink Paper* reported that 33 people were arrested.[419] Issue 13 of the *Pink Paper* notes that the LGTG had organised a one-day event on 12 March for youth workers, teachers and teenagers to discuss clause 28.[420]

Clause 28 galvanised gay and lesbian opposition and the organisation Stonewall was born out of that. But the legislation preventing the promotion of homosexuality was passed. The Local Government Act 1988 section 28 stated that 'A local authority shall not— (a) intentionally promote homosexuality or publish material with the intention of promoting homosexuality; (b) promote the teaching in any maintained school of the acceptability of homosexuality as a pretended family relationship'.

The Association of Local Authorities (17 London authorities) sought legal advice on section 28 Local Government Act. Counsel's view was that 'youth organisations which provide social and welfare facilities for young people who are, or believe they may be, gay or lesbian are not promoting homosexuality'.[421]

Such legal advice was a relief to groups such as the London Gay Teenage Group, as it continued to support many gay and lesbian teenagers. However, Kensington Council refused a grant to the Notting Hill Lesbian and Gay Youth Group in 1989 based on section 28.[422]

Anthony Hillin recalled:

At the LGTG we didn't stop any of the group's activities in response to Section 28 but we were careful how we described them. Much of the work around safer sex education was defined as HIV prevention and social skills development. Members answering the helpline understood they should be wary that some calls might be placed by the press or others checking up on the LGTG or even be taped and monitored by the authorities. They were careful to emphasise the group's age limits, that it was a social support group and to be wary of questions about sex. The standard spiel included things like 'Because of Section 28 we can't promote homosexuality or gay sex. If you were to be sexual you need to be aware of the age of consent and keeping yourself safe, including HIV. The LGTG provides a place to meet other young gay people, to talk and feel supported'.[423]

James Byrne attended the group between 1986 and 1988. In 2020 he recalled:

I can very well remember my first trip to the teenage group, I was shy and nervous, like so many before and after me. I recall immediately feeling a connection with Anthony Hillin, the youth worker, and appreciated the nurturing environment Anthony created within the group. In a matter of weeks, again, like so many before and after, I became more confident, made new friends, and became very involved in the group... people blossomed within the group. I have often said to others that young vulnerable people would turn up at the group (or we would go out to first meet them somewhere off-site) feeling dispirited, disheartened, depressed, distressed and afraid and, within weeks, they would be laughing, joyous, confident, vibrant and proud and comfortable with who they were. Being part of this process is what makes me proud of my time at the London Gay Teenage Group, especially as it was so desperately needed back then... the teenage group was essentially like any other youth group you might have visited at the time. We had a table football machine and we often played rounders on the green outside. To a casual observer it was simply a youth group, and that was the beauty of it. Only if you looked a bit harder, and listened intently, might you work out that the young men and women seemed to be all gay. It was a place that young people could go and, unlike the regular gay scene, continue to be young and not have to grow up too quickly. I realise that probably sounds a bit quaint and possibly naïve but I really felt that it allowed young gay men and women the opportunity to continue to do the things that their straight peers were doing AND simultaneously safely come to terms with their sexuality in a time when, without the internet and with different prevailing attitudes, this was often more difficult. Adding in the safer sex education, self-esteem building and all of the other great things brought to the group to help us all stay healthy physically, emotionally and psychologically, made it a truly special place. I think that the discussions on safer sex and the focus on building up self-esteem may well have saved lives. A lot of people coming to the group for the first time were in very dark place emotionally and, without the support of the group, they may otherwise have had suicidal thoughts and/or engaged in unsafe sex in situations where they were being exploited... I think most of us felt like we were part of something and that the group looked after each and every one of us. Whatever was happening at home, at work or at school, the group was our refuge on Wednesday evenings and Sunday afternoons.[424]

The group had residential weekends away aiming to develop members skills in peer counselling, peer safer sex education and self-esteem. James recalled those weekends:

I recall on one trip listening to a really nice young man, in his early twenties, telling us that he was suffering from ARC (Aids-Related Complex, as it was then known). To this day, when I recall that session (and I periodically do), it still hurts. He was such a lovely sweet charming guy and I was shocked by his situation and his candour. In particular, I remember how selfless he was, his primary concern was that others should not find themselves in his situation. He was upbeat and vibrant in spite of everything, he was so brave, at least on the outside. I don't know what became of him but, sadly, I can guess.[425]

Anthony Hillin, the lead part-time youth worker, brought considerable counselling and support skills to the group:

A lot of attention was given to psychological and emotional safety, especially at the start and finish of individual counselling and group discussions. We started by encouraging members not to feel pressured to share information they didn't feel ready to, nor to participate in ways that didn't feel right for them. We ended by encouraging them to seek support when needed and reminded them about self-help and coping strategies. It was important to allow adequate time to conclude, especially if the session involved strong emotional responses.

The group's membership was strikingly diverse across a myriad of dimensions: race, ethnicity, social class, political views, stage of gay identity formation, personality, and comfort with camp, effeminate or macho traits or behaviour. The age range of sixteen to twenty-one could involve significant gulfs in maturity. A sixteen-year-old might typically be at school and living with parents whereas a twenty-one-year-old might be more independent in their living and financial arrangements. Psychosocial development wasn't always correlated with chronological age. Some 16-year-olds were very worldly, perhaps living independently having fled a difficult home environment. Some 21-year-olds were at an early stage of accepting their sexual orientation. Many had not previously encountered such diversity. As would be expected, occasionally these vast differences lead to friction but it was usually mild. What was remarkable was the readiness of members to embrace diversity.

These formal group discussions helped bridge differences by fostering connections within the group. Existing bonds were deepened and new ones created between members who had not previously felt connected. Tensions were eased – someone previously viewed as irritating, aloof or extreme in their political correctness or lack thereof, might be seen more compassionately, or even with affection, when we know more of their story.[426]

The LGYM appears to have folded about 1988. This was not a consequence of section 28, rather the absence of any individuals aged under 26 to take up the organising work required to keep it going. As Martin Collins mentioned (quoted earlier):

When we passed our 26th birthdays, I think the organisation (LGYM) died, maybe 1988 ish at a guess… Knowing the anarchistic way things were run, I very much doubt if there was any archive saved. I don't even remember a bank account.[427]

A Lesbian and Gay Youth Federation (LGYF) was set up to coordinate and consult between gay youth groups. It produced a publication called *Pink*

Promotion in 1988. Maybe this replaced the LGYM? Neither left much archive evidence, or at least any that has come to light to date (2020).

Opposition to clause 28/section 28 led to widespread activity resulting not only in the creation of the Stonewall Organisation. A group called Lesbian and Gay Youth Action (LAGYAG) was also established in 1988.[428]

The Queen Mother, as Patron, visited the Manor Gardens Centre in March 1988. She was presented with the four research booklets produced by the LGTG. They were handed to her by James Byrne and Ayo Brown.[429] The Queen Mother had been a patron of the Manor Gardens Centre since 1926. James Byrne recalled the visit:

> She was very elderly then and, although she looked well, she was definitely wearing an awful lot of make-up. She moved down the line and the various people before me introduced themselves and presented her with a token of some sort. When she got to me I told her that I represented the London Lesbian and Gay Teenage Group. I remember her saying 'very good' and taking the book from me and moving on. As with all of the items presented to her, the book was quickly taken from her hand and carried by one of the entourage. I have always wondered if she really understood who I was, what I was representing and if she ever turned the pages of the book I gave her. I'd like to think she did.[430]

Some members of LGTG appeared on Channel 4's *Network 7* in 1988, including Paul Harvey, then 17, a trainee chef from Shropshire, who had run away to London and was taken into care. His father was a policeman. Jason, from Dundee, also said a few words on the programme. The *Network 7* programme featured four different people coming out live on TV to their friends and in one case, Lisa Howard from Devon, came out to her nephew.

The International Lesbian and Gay Youth Conference was held in Berlin 30 July to 7 August 1988. In December 1988 a support group for young people affected or infected with HIV was established. The Positive Young Gay Group was coordinated by the NLL.

Chapter Fifteen

BUTTERFLIES EMERGE AND FLY, 1989

I have often told others about the transformative power that the group had for members, including holding up the LGTG as a glowing example in my subsequent work. I've used a similar metaphor, thinking of many as butterflies emerging from the chrysalis of being downcast, depressed, anxious and sometimes self-loathing and suicidal. It was so moving and such a pleasure to see how rapidly members would spread their beautiful wings and fly.

(Anthony Hillin, Youth Worker at the LGTG)

A nthony Hillin wrote a two-part article in *Capital Gay* entitled 'Our Youth Are Our Future'. In the article he discusses the low self-esteem of many young gay and lesbian people, and that 'damaged self-esteem makes young gay men particularly vulnerable to HIV infection'. Anthony described how there was a need for a holistic approach to safer sex education. He points out that many young gay men feel a pressure to be sexual when what they really wanted was a cuddle, someone to talk with and not to sleep alone. In essence to be loved in a gay way. He organised weekends for the LGTG where these issues could be discussed and self-esteem explored, as well as having fun. The weekends also aimed to develop the young people as 'bare-foot' sex educators, spreading messages to their peer group. 'A culture of loving and supportive brotherhood has been built by mutual and genuine appreciation, sharing of members' stories of pain and joy, celebrating each other's steps forward and vigilantly watching for manifestations of internalised oppression such as criticisms, put-downs, low-expectations etc.'[431]

The dangers of HIV infection were the subject of a chapter by Douglas Feldman, writing about North America in *Gay and Lesbian Youth* (edited by Herdt, 1989). Feldman wrote that:

Teenagers in general are fairly ill-informed about AIDS and safe sex practices... It is also likely that this lack of adequate information translates into unsafe sex practices. While the American gay community has undergone a major social revolution in strongly embracing the condom as a central tool in safer sex encounters (an object of sharp derision only a few years ago), it is not clear if gay and bisexual teenagers are also using condoms in any significant numbers.[432]

Shaun Hanson recalled his six months at the group which was in 1989:

I was 21 (the age limit of the group) when I was chairman in 1989. My secretary was Jason Richer. We met Wednesdays and Sundays. We would spend an hour or two playing pool and other games. A social setting like a youth club. After that, we would go to The Black Cap in Camden on Wednesdays, and to Benjy's in Mile End on Sundays. The youngest member of the group was 12 and he was a boy that wanted to be a girl. I don't think any of us could fully help him with that but he was very happy to be accepted by all of us and mingled in the same way as anyone else. We got advance permission from The Black Cap and Benjy's to enter their premises as long as everyone behaved (which was challenging) and soft drinks only. Our funding was of a grant from Islington Council which was always threatened... At the time, I lived in Hastings and I would take the train on each occasion. I have no doubt that I became aware of the group through a listing in *Gay Times* magazine.[433]

The reference by Shaun to the boy who wanted to be a girl is one of the few recollections uncovered in this research of a young person attending the group who today might identify as transgender. In the '70s and '80s the term transgender did not exist. We knew about transvestites (cross dressers) and also a few people who'd had a sex change (transsexual was the term used then). But the two should not be confused.

Jayne County, a rock singer from the USA, who had been Wayne County, visited the group in 1978 while undergoing transition from male to female.[434]

Two transvestites, Sue and Joanne, from London Friend, visited the group in 1979, but only a few people took the opportunity to talk with them.[435] Some of the young people who attended the LGTG may have later changed their sex and having attended the group as male are now female or vice versa. In research for this book only two cases have been identified.

A number of men who attended the LGTG have been, or are, involved in drag, performing as women, but retaining their male 'daytime' identity. One such person featured in the *Pink Paper*. In April 1989 the paper reported on a near fatal fall from a great height by David, known as 'Camp David'. David Close, aged 24, former LGTG member, was in hospital after a fall of 120 feet in a suicide leap. He recovered and returned to performing drag.[436]

The 6th Annual Conference of the International Lesbian and Gay Youth Organisation was held in Kobenhaven (Copenhagen), Denmark, from 30 July to 3 August. It was advertised as a Lesbian, Gay and Bisexual Youth Conference on Sexuality.

In the autumn a new gay youth group for under-21-year-olds was established in Hammersmith and Fulham. It was called 'Out on Thursday'.[437]

Camden allocated 12 part-time youth worker hours to develop a Young Black Lesbian Group. The following year this group went on a trip to Holland.

North London Line moved from their premises in Highbury Station Road.[438]

Chapter Sixteen

INNER LONDON EDUCATION AUTHORITY ABOLISHED, 1990

The Notting Hill Lesbian and Gay Youth Group (catering for those up to age 25) had to agree to drop the Lesbian and Gay Youth part of its title in order to receive a grant of £950 from the local council. The previous year it was denied a grant because of section 28.[439]

In Hull the Northern Theatre Company produced a play called *Love Kevin* with a cast of gay teenagers, including a 13-year-old boy. The play, written by Richard Green, dealt with teenage prostitution, being gay and drug-taking. Hull City Council considered use of section 28 to ban the play. The theatre company turned itself into a private theatre club to avoid possible prosecution, and insisted all the parents of the teenagers involved in the production had given permission for their children to be involved in the play. It was due to be performed at the company's venue in Madeley Street, Hull on 26 January 1990.[440]

Stepping Out, the newest lesbian and gay youth group for London's under-25-year-olds (no lower age limit), was launched at the London Lesbian and Gay Centre in February.[441]

Lesbian and Gay Issues in the Classroom by Simon Harris was published by the Open University Press. Most of the material in the book was written between 1985–86, when Harris was a student on a Postgraduate Certificate in Education (PGCE) course in Cambridge. He stated that a large part of the information and ideas in his original work became obsolete by changes, such as the appearance on the statute book of section 28 of the Local Government Act 1988. Other changes also affecting the material, were the transfer of responsibility for sex education to school governing bodies, and a better understanding of the transmission of HIV.

ILEA was abolished in 1990. Their education functions were handed over to the individual London boroughs.

The age of consent for gay male sex was still 21.

Chapter Seventeen

THE END OF THE CENTURY, 1991–2000

In 1991 Luton Young Gay and Lesbian Group for under-25-year-olds won official backing from Bedfordshire County Council. This angered the Member of Parliament for North Luton, John Carlisle. He said it was utterly distasteful.[442] In 1992 gay and lesbian teenagers protested at the House of Commons by dropping their trousers.[443]

Hackney had a gay and lesbian teenage youth group called 'Staying Out'.[444] Richard Collumbell went along in 1994: 'I first went in the summer of 1994, and kept going until at least 1997. It was good. Had a better venue than [the London] Teenage Group. In their notices someone mentioned there was a course on lesbian and gay history and culture running at the Teenage Group which is how I ended up going there too'.[445]

In April 1992 the *Pink Paper* listed an Islington social/activities group for Gay Young Men 16–25 meeting at the old Fire Station, 84 Mayton Street, off Seven Sisters Road.[446]

While the Borough of Islington was at the forefront, along with Camden and other boroughs, of advancing provision for gay and lesbian teenagers, tackling sexism and promoting diversity, there was a darker side to the borough at the time. The council's laissez-faire attitude to the way children in their care were managed and the clear exploitation of some children by a number of predatory adults, both heterosexual and homosexual, eventually led to allegations of a cover-up.

The vetting of personnel working with children had been addressed by the Home Office and the DHSS in 'Protection of Children: Disclosure of criminal background of those with access to children' (1985) but the report by Dixon to ILEA in 1987, discussed in Chapter Thirteen, highlighted that many gay and lesbian people were criminalised for matters not subject to criminal law if heterosexual (such as kissing in the street which could lead to an indecency charge). It is not known if the Borough of Islington employed individuals who would have been vetted out elsewhere for homosexual offences. It is clear that some individuals exploited Islington's weaknesses in child protection which may have arisen from a political stance that was anti-police and pro-gay and -lesbian.

On 7 October 1992 the *Evening Standard* published a report featuring the case of a child abused in the care of Islington Council where the council hindered the police investigation.[447] In the 1990s a series of allegations were made that children in care in the Borough of Islington in the 1980s had been abused and that the abuse was not properly investigated. In addition, staff who were dismissed for allegations of misconduct with young people often went on to work with children for other authorities as the council generally had a policy of not involving the police. In 1995 the council commissioned a report to investigate these allegations. Former social worker Michael Rosenbaum took the council to an industrial tribunal for unfair dismissal claiming he was dismissed for exposing sex abuse in the borough's children's homes in the 1980s.[448]

The White Report was a report commissioned by Islington Council in 1995 following serious allegations about childcare practices in the borough. The allegations had been made principally by the *Evening Standard.* The allegations were investigated by Ian A White CBE MSc (then Director of Social Services for Oxfordshire County Council) and Kate Hart MSc CQSW (Principal Officer, Oxfordshire County Council) who completed their 'Report of the Inquiry into the management of child care in the London Borough of Islington, The White Report' in May 1995. Survivors of abuse in the borough's children's homes were still pursuing claims for compensation in 2019, although over £2 million had been paid out by the summer of 2019.[449]

In 1993 a group of gay youths in Liverpool were filmed by Sandi Hughes. The youths answer questions about their lives while sitting around in what appears to be the meeting place of Friend, Merseyside. The Gay Youth Group met on Wednesday evenings.[450]

On Saturday 7 May 1994, outside Charing Cross Police Station, a group of gay teenagers aged 16–18 publicly admitted to having gay sex and challenged the police to arrest them. No-one was arrested. This event was referred to as the 'Teenage Turn In' by radical activists called 'Outrage!'

The 1994 International Lesbian and Gay Youth Conference held in Ireland, was reported on Channel 4's TV programme *OUT*.[451]

In 1994 Parliament lowered the age of consent for gay sex to 18. Edwina

Currie (Conservative MP) wanted it to be 16, and tabled an amendment to that effect, but failed to win enough support. The Conservative Party was the government of the day, with John Major as Prime Minister. Many gay and lesbian people demonstrated outside the Houses of Parliament on the night of the debate, expressing their dissatisfaction at the law still remaining two years higher than for consenting heterosexual sexual activity.[452]

Shropshire County Youth Service offered support for gay and lesbian teenagers. They advertised in the *Shropshire Star* for a paid and a volunteer youth worker to befriend lesbian and gay young people aged 14–20 who attended a Telford youth centre. One parent objected when her 15-year-old son started attending the group as a gay teenager. A 19-year-old salesman and three youth workers befriended the boy. His mother found safer sex advice for gay men in her son's bedroom along with condoms. She sought and obtained a county court injunction to prevent the four persons having any contact with the boy until he was 18 (the new age of consent for gay men).[453] The case highlights the difficulties of working with children under 16 (as it is now) in groups which also include older youths.

It seems that the objections of the parent led Shropshire Council to close down the Telford Lesbian and Gay Youth Group in November 1994, while they investigated whether their financial support for the group contravened section 28 of the Local Government Act. In April 1995 the council announced the group could reopen as they were not breaking the law. The group catered for young people aged between 14 and 21.[454]

PACE (Project for Advice, Counselling and Education) had started in the mid-1980s. As Richard Desmond recalled: 'They started at the LLGC … in Islington but after funding cuts happened they moved to King's Cross and then folded about three years ago [2015]. They ran a youth group at Jacksons Lane Arts Centre on Highgate Hill which I believe took over from LGTG'.[455]

In June 1996 it was announced that a West Country gay youth group called Freedom had been awarded a National Lotteries Board grant of £159,000 to set up a housing project, a helpline and employ a full-time youth worker. Freedom covered Bristol, Bath and much of the rest of Somerset.[456]

Over 1996–97 Sarah Cundy was researching 'Growing Up Gay in Britain and America: A Comparative Study on the Effects of Growing Up in an Identity Against which the Law Discriminates and How Some Individuals Successfully Negotiate the Process'. Cundy had received a Fox Fellowship to do this research in USA. Earlier she had been working on the study of gay teenagers growing up whilst based in Cambridge, UK.[457]

In 1997 the Scout Association lifted its ban on gay people serving as Scout leaders. John Fogg of the Scout Association said that 'no young person or adult should receive less favourable treatment because of their sexuality, gender, marital status or ethnic origin'.[458]

The LGTG was still going in the late 1990s and produced a magazine called *Next Generation*. Financial support came from Islington Council. As Richard Collumbell recalled:

> We had to apply every year for a grant from Islington Council. The grant covered most, but not all, of our rent payable to Manor Gardens, so we were always in arrears, and we had to do regular fund-raising to cover the cost. This was mostly done via collecting tins going round gay bars in Soho. The two editions of the magazine we did brought in quite a bit of money too.[459]

In 1998 the group had to deal with a youth worker who had slept with one of the members. This was brought to the attention of the committee and as a result the youth worker resigned. Richard Collumbell was chair at the time and accepted the youth worker's resignation.[460]

In 1998 the group had included the word bisexual in their title: London Lesbian Gay and Bisexual Teenage Group. Their magazine had been distributed to over 350 youth groups affiliated to the London Union of Youth Clubs.[461] As to what happened to the group after Richard left no-one really knows. Or at least no-one has come forward to explain what happened.[462]

In 1998 the City of Liverpool Council were advertising for two part-time 'Lesbian/Bisexual Young Women Workers' for 'Gay Youth R Out ... to develop work primarily with Young Lesbian/Bisexual Women within a long established gay youth project'.[463]

In 1999 15-year-old Nathan Maloney, played by Charlie Hunnam (himself aged 19 at the time), arrived on the TV screen in *Queer as Folk*. Broadcast on Channel 4, this drama, created by Russell T Davies, smashed all previous restrictions on depicting a gay teenager. Sexually explicit and challenging moral boundaries, the programme must have been a godsend to many young gay men. Finally gay youth had truly arrived on the screen.[464]

As we moved into the 21st century openly gay teenagers were certainly more numerous and better catered for than 30 years earlier. But those aged 16 and 17 were still not on a legally equal footing with heterosexual peers. And sexual education in schools rarely was inclusive of gay and lesbian teenagers.

Appendix 1

GAY YOUTH WORKERS

In the mid-1970s a few gay youth workers, including Chris Heaume, were beginning to organise and campaign for provision for gay young people and gay rights in the youth service. The first meeting of the youth workers is recorded as being 13 December 1976.[465] At that time the group had no name. It subsequently chose the name SAYS (Sexual Awareness in the Youth Service). 'I think it came out of sexuality awareness training I and others were doing then at the YMCA youth workers college in Walthamstow'.[466]

Chris Heaume grew up in Guernsey. He trained in youth work in Exeter and went on to work for the youth service in Newham, Islington, Camden and Tower Hamlets, and was CEO of Central London Connexions from 2002 to 2013.[467] He was on the development team for *Nighthawks*, a film by Ron Peck, released in 1978, about a gay teacher coming out. Chris appeared in the sequel film *Strip Jack Naked* (1991), made with the outtakes from *Nighthawks*. Both films were products of the 4 Corner Film Workshop in Hackney. Chris was seconded at the end of 1989 for a year to the National Youth Bureau to develop a youth work curriculum. Chris was awarded an OBE in 2007.[468]

As Chris explained, regarding training youth workers: 'we wanted a platform that was wider than homosexualities, to include sexualities, sexism, work with boys and masculinity. It was to challenge the social norms and open up better practice'.[469]

Those present at the first meeting on 13 December 1976 included Chris Heaume, Ric Rogers, Dennis Wester, Philip Hawkins, John Hoyland and Michael Trotter. Present at the second meeting in London in January 1977 were Dave Randall, Gilly Salvat, Fred Wilenius, Phil Hawkins, Chris Heaume and Ric Rogers. London Council of Social Services offered secretarial support to the group. Motions were prepared for the Community and Youth Service Association Conference. A leaflet, 'Does the Youth Service want you if you are gay?', was produced and circulated by the Community and Youth Service Association (CYSA). Members of the SAYS and gay youth workers group socialised together at the MM Club in Munster Square, NW 1.[470]

In June 1977 the Education and Training Officer for the NAYC wrote to all local divisions and associations outlining the NAYC support for the findings of the NCVYS report on young people and homosexuality. The National Executive Committee of the NAYC also at that time supported a reduction of the age of consent for homosexual men to 18 (although the Members' National Conference supported a reduction to the age of 16). The letter calls for training of youth workers in issues of sexuality and greater provision for young people experiencing psychosexual problems. The letter refers to the support available from Chris Heaume (an ILEA youth worker) with advice, and that Chris has a list of 35 youth workers in various parts of the country who can help.[471]

Three members of SAYS attended the CYSA Conference in Belfast in April 1977, where a motion supporting gay rights was passed by the conference.[472]

By 1978 SAYS and Gay Youth Workers Group were using headed letter paper (something called for at previous meetings). Meetings were by now held at the London Council of Social Services, 68 Chalton Street, London NW 1.[473] Chris Heaume worked as a detached youth worker in Kentish Town from January 1977 to December 1982 and during that time the group often met at his office: 4 Caversham Road.

In 1977 the National Council for Civil Liberties conducted research into 'homosexuality and the social services'. Some councils refused employment in jobs connected to children simply because the applicant was gay. But most council social services departments trusted homosexuals to work with children in care (Ferris, 1977).

The legal position of adults working with gay teenagers was explored to avoid any possible prosecution for inciting underage homosexual activity. Gay youth workers were vulnerable along with teachers, and anyone working with children. Richard McMullen, a gay youth worker at the Third Feathers Club in Earl's Court, was sacked in 1980.[474] He felt it was because he was openly gay, but the authorities gave other reasons. *Capital Gay* reported in January 1982 that he was still out of work. He turned his hand to writing. In 1990 *Enchanted Youth* was published. This was a follow-up to *Enchanted Boy*. Both examine issues of abuse and prostitution, issues McMullen dealt with in earlier years working at Centrepoint, and which later he was involved in with 'Streetwise'.[475]

In 1981 CHE released a report about discrimination at work. *What about the gay workers: a report of the Commission on Discrimination* included eight well-known cases (Clews, 2017).

In 1982 youth worker Judith Williams was sacked. It was claimed this was because she was open about being a lesbian.[476]

Minutes of a gay youth work group, held in September 1983, record that Bob Crossman (vice-chair of ILEA Equal Opportunities Sub-Committee and Borough of Islington member on ILEA) explained to the meeting what was being done on equal opportunities within ILEA regarding gay and lesbian issues. Crossman had been in discussion with the Principal Equal Opportunities Officer, who had stated her pragmatic and moral objections to homosexuality as an equal opportunity issue.[477] In November 1983 a meeting for gays and lesbians working with young people in the social services, probation service, youth service and prison service was held in Kentish Town.[478]

In 1984 Rugby Council removed sexual orientation from their equal opportunities policy and made it clear that openly gay and lesbian people would not be employed by the council.

In 1985 Lorraine Trenchard and Hugh Warren, of the LGTG Research project, produced a booklet *Talking about Youth Work*. This was essentially a guide for all youth workers and, in particular, those who had little knowledge of gay and lesbian teenagers.

Within ILEA a Lesbian and Gay Youth Workers Group was set up. The secretary was based in Ealing and the group met every four to six weeks at various venues.[479]

In 1988 two national conferences were held for lesbian and gay youth workers. The first focused on section 28. The second conference centred around the idea of setting up a national organisation of lesbian and gay youth and community workers. The National Organisation of Lesbian and Gay Youth and Community Workers (NOLGYCW) was established as a result. NOLGYCW set out to operate on three fronts: personal, professional and political.[480]

Openly gay and lesbian youth workers were still vulnerable. Many gay and lesbian youth workers remained in the closet at work well into the 21st century. As Chris Heaume pointed out in 2020, it was also very difficult for senior youth officials to be open as well:

the time was very different from now; it was odd enough for a youth worker to be openly gay, but for an officer [Council Youth Services Officer] it would have been unheard of. We were all concerned about the security of our jobs, etc. plus the vigorous assumption that the words 'gay' and 'youth' and 'work' spelt criminality, up to no good etc. We presumed it would make us unemployable.[481]

Some of those young people who attended the LGTG went on to become youth workers. Notably Maureen Hand, Steve Power and John Stevens.

It is fitting to pay tribute to all youth workers who have supported young people. As Chris Heaume stated in 2020:

Professionally aligned to education, youth work helps young people get the maximum from life. Detached youth workers have no buildings, but reach-out to isolated or alienated young people in their own communities. Others work in schools, colleges or youth centres giving young people a leg-up to solutions, ways forward – advising, suggesting, cajoling, listening, helping, representing, referring to specialists – not just driving minibuses or playing pool! Young people can't walk away from most authority figures without causing an issue. They can walk away from youth workers. They hold the power and reap the rewards.

Youth work has sometimes played an important role helping young gay and lesbian people to build their own groups, fit for what they need, through the rocky early days, to becoming established, adding continuity and consistency to build a secure base, a leadership team, a place in both the gay and the youth work communities, and safety and friendship to young gay people. It has also helped more widely in the youth services to open the eyes of young people to the realities of being gay.[482]

Appendix 2

AGE OF CONSENT

Equal age of consent for homosexual acts with heterosexual acts finally became law in England and Wales by the passing of the Sexual Offences Amendment Act 2000. This became law on 8 January 2001. In Northern Ireland the age was set at 17 until it was lowered to 16 in 2009. The Sexual Offences (Amendment) Act 2000 also introduced the new offence of 'having sexual intercourse or engaging in any other sexual activity with a person under 18 if in a position of trust in relation to that person'.

Appendix 3

TABLE OF KNOWN OFFICE HOLDERS OF THE GROUP, 1977–2000

	Chair	Secretary	Treasurer
1977	Steve Power	Robert Halls	Paul Welch?
1978	Steve Power	Robert Halls Andrew Martin	Neville Magee
1979	Steve Power	John Stevens Andrew Martin	Tony Baker
1980	Steve Power (till June) Gary Barker	Andrew Martin Leslie Wimpory	Alan Williams Martin J Collins
1981	Gary Barker (till August) Jain Clarke	Derek Bonner (from 3 August–9 September '81) Philip Martin (from 9 September '81–9 November '81)[1]	Martin J Collins
1982	Jain Clarke Sarah Wilkinson	Claude Christian Simon Bulpin (October '82)	Martin J Collins[2] Paul Williams (October '82)
1983	David Joad (from February '83–October '84)	Christopher Lloyd Neil Ridley (February '83–) Graham Yelland (October '83–February '84)	Keith Herman (March '83) Bob Webber (September '83–June '84)

---

1 Both Tom Howarth and Philip Howarth were also secretary at some point, according to the Annual Report 1982–83.
2 Stayed on as advisor to treasurer.

1984	David Joad Steve R Lunniss (from October)	Graham Yelland Jamie Styles (February 84–)	Owen Vernon? (fundraiser) Alan McHugh
1985	Steve R Lunniss	Jamie Styles Barbara Hercules-Joseph (October 85–March 86)	Wayne Brimmer Neil Spencer
1986	Steve R Lunniss Julian Faisal (from April) Brian Healey/Nick Stanislaus (co-chairs from November)	Mark Dakin (from April) Steve Erwood Chris Gabel (from November)	Neil Spencer Graham Yelland/ Barry Lewis (from June)
1987	Brian Healey/Nick Stanislaus (co-chairs) James Byrne	Chris Gabel Barry Lewis	Ralph Nadal
1988	James Byrne Robert?	Barry Lewis	
1989	Shaun Hanson Paul Jordan Michael Meleady	Jason Richer Ian Hemming	Jason Richer (from September)
1990			
1991			
1992			
1993			
1994			
1995			
1996	Anthony?		
1997	Richard Collumbell		
1998	Richard Collumbell		
1999	Salvador Lloret-Farina		
2000	Myles?		

Based on archive available including minutes of meetings and annual reports. Question marks are shown if the information has not been confirmed.

Select Bibliography

Clews, Colin (2017) *Gay in the 80s* (Matador Books: Leicester)

Coles, Richard (2014) *Fathomless Riches: Or How I Went from Pop to Pulpit* (Weidenfeld and Nicolson: London)

Feather, Stuart (2015) *Blowing the Lid: Gay Liberation, Sexual Revolution and Radical Queens* (Zero Books: Winchester)

Ferris, Dave (1977) *Homosexuality and the Social Services* (NCCL: London)

Grey, Antony (1992) *Quest for Justice: Towards Homosexual Emancipation* (Sinclair-Stevenson: London)

Harris, Simon (1990) *Lesbian and Gay Issues in the English Classroom* (Open University Press: Buckingham)

Herdt, Gilbert (ed.) (1989) *Gay and Lesbian Youth* (Harrington Park Press: New York/London)

Joint Council for Gay Teenagers (1980) *I Know What I Am: Gay Teenagers and the Law* (JCGT: London)

Joint Council for Gay Teenagers (edited by Burbidge, Michael and Walters, Jonathan) (1981) *Breaking the Silence: Gay Teenagers Speak for Themselves* (JCGT: London)

Norris, Stephanie and Read, Emma (1985) *Out: Out in the Open: People Talking About Being Gay or Bisexual* (Pan: London)

Power, Lisa (1995) *No Bath But Plenty of Bubbles: An Oral History of the Gay Liberation Front 1970–73* (Cassell: London)

Rees, David (1982) *The Milkman's on His Way* (Gay Men's Press: London)

Scott-Presland, Peter (2015) *Amiable Warriors: A History of the Campaign for Homosexual Equality and Its Times, Volume 1: A Space to Breathe* (Paradise Press: London)

Trenchard, Lorraine and Warren, Hugh (1984) *Something to tell you* (London Gay Teenage Group: London)

Trenchard, Lorraine (1984) *Talking about Young Lesbians* (London Gay Teenage Group: London)

Trenchard, Lorraine and Warren, Hugh (1985) *Talking about Youth Work* (London Gay Teenage Group: London)

Warren, Hugh (1984) *Talking about School* (London Gay Teenage Group: London)

Weeks, Jeffrey (2016) *Coming Out: The Emergence of LGBT Identities in Britain from the 19th Century to the Present* (40th Anniversary Edition) (Quartet: London)

Carol Jones and Pat Mahony (1989) *Learning Our Lines: Sexuality and Social Control in Education* (The Women's Press) has a chapter on the Young Lesbian Group.

Steve Power was interviewed by Jeffrey Weeks as part of an Open University television programme connected to a social science course. It was first broadcast in 1980. The interview is available on YouTube.

In July 2019 some former members of the LGTG/LLGTG held a reunion picnic in London. Twenty-one people attended. It is hoped a similar event can be held in the future.

If you were in the LGTG you might like to join the closed Facebook group: London Lesbian & Gay Teenage Group memories 1976–2000.

Endnotes

1   The modern vogue of the term queer, as in queer art, queer people, queer history etc., is something the author has not felt comfortable with. Gay is much more acceptable. It encompassed all elements of the 'LGBT' spectrum when it was used in the 1970s and only later was its use for men only.

2   *Daily Telegraph*, 8 March 1976, 'Gay News in Library angers councillor'.

3   Described by John Hart in the television programme 'Male Sexuality', an episode of the London Weekend Television series *Gay Life* (1981). He talked of the competitive and aggressive nature of cruising, reinforcing the view of men as masculine. He also spoke of casual sex inhibiting the building up of good relationships. The episode is available on YouTube: https://www.youtube.com/watch?v=GFGxzKyFzcM (accessed 4 July 2021).

4   Author of the history of CHE, *Amiable Warriors, Volume 1: A Space to Breathe*, 2015.

5   *Birmingham Daily Post*, 12 September 1962, 'Wanted bus at the Gay Youth Centre'.

6   *Rugby Advertiser*, 5 September 1950, 'A G.A.Y. Birthday: The Rugby branch of the Guild of Abstaining Youth celebrated its first birthday with a tea and a suitably inscribed iced birthday cake'.

7   *Wolverhampton Express and Star*, 8 January 1968.

8   Grey (1992) p160.

9   Scott-Presland (2015) p274.

10 Ibid, pp272–6.

11 Ibid, p277.

12   *Birmingham Post*, 10 April 1968, page 11 'Youths conduct wrong'. See also, Tony Geraghty's report in *The Sunday Times*, 17 March 1968: 'The disturbing case of the consenting teenagers', which covers events leading up to the case in Stafford Assize Court and also the death in October 1967 of 19-year-old William Ansell, of Stoke-on-Trent, who hanged himself in his cell. The two reports appear to conflict as the *Birmingham Post* states four youths were sentenced at the Appeal hearing, whereas *The Sunday Times* article states only three youths were sentenced (initially on 6 February); the 19-year-old having hanged himself on 20 October at Risley Remand Centre. Was it possible the Appeal Court heard an appeal by the dead teenager?

13   HCA/ALBANYTRUST/14/127, letter Antony Grey to David Hepworth Public Health Department, 10 April 1969 and reply 22 April.

14   HCA/ALBANYTRUST/14/127, letter Mrs C F Cordell to Dr J Orme, 2 June 1969.

15   HCA/ALBANYTRUST/14/127, letter Dr Orme to Mrs Cordell, 9 June 1969.

16   *GN* issue 123, 14 July 1977. See also pp16–19 in *Out* by Norris and Read (1985).

17   *The Observer*, 6 May 1973. Alongside the article was an advert, 'Gay Young Maternities; so delightfully different', featuring maternity clothing from Maternelle shops in Knightsbridge and Marylebone High Street!

18   *Sunday Times*, 28 October 1973. Bates, John E and Bentler, P M, 'Play Activities of Normal and Effeminate Boys', *Developmental Psychology*, 9, 1, 20–27, July 1973.

19   Steve Power email to author, 3 February 2019.

20   *GN* issue 45, 25 April–8 May 1974.

21   HCA/Beach/4.

22   Power (1995) p110, and p335: Tony Reynolds died of an AIDS-related illness. According to Feather (2015) p182; Alaric Sumner's mother heard of GLF and told her son to join!

23   Nettie Pollard attended one GLF Youth Group meeting. '…it was at someone's parents' house in Lady Margaret Road, Tufnell Park. I think there was someone else 21 or over making their sole visit. He asked about the only under-21s and was told "we don't want any sparrow hawks round here". There were about 12 people, male and female, and some looked about 13 or 14. There was some discussion about how

even a reduction of the age of consent to 16, wouldn't help everyone/ all gay youth. Very assertive discussion about the Youth Group issue of *Come Together*, plans for a demonstration. And someone talked about how many famous historical figures were gay, lesbian or bi. Remember Alexander the Great being mentioned. A 16-year-old boy who was squatting said how difficult it was as you couldn't get benefits at 16. He said you always have to cheat on public transport. A very warm and welcoming atmosphere at the meeting. I'm glad they allowed me to visit' (email to author, 17 January 2020).

24   *Come Together*, issue 8, the leafleting of the Union pub in South London is mentioned. In HCA/Journals/2536.

25   *Come Together*, issue 10, November 1971. HCA/Journals/2536.

26   The programme in HCA/Beach/4.

27   HCA/Journals/280D.

28   HCA/Journals/2536, *Come Together*, issue 12, 1972.

29   *GN* issue 46, 1974.

30   *GN* issue 44, April 11–24 1974.

31   *Surrey Daily Advertiser*, 12 August 1977, 'Sex booklet angers youth leaders' (LAGNA) and *GN* issue 127, 22 September 1977, 'Youth leaders renew attack on gay advice'.

32   *GN*, issue 4.

33   HCA/CHE2/9/47.

34   Scott-Presland (2015) p271.

35   Trevor Locke email to author, 8 November 2020.

36   *Birmingham Daily Post*, 5 April 1973, 'Students urged to aid "gay" societies'.

37   Scott-Presland (2015) p445.

38   Scott-Presland (2015) Chapter 4. Paul Temperton went on to become General Secretary of CHE.

39   Ibid, p575.

40   Issue 12 was an 'unauthorised edition' put out by a few members in defiance of a think-in on 15 March 1972.

41   Op cit, p573.

42   Scott-Presland (2015) p370.

43   HCA/CHE/7/14/A.

44   *GN*, issue 64, 13–26 February 1975.

45   Notes of meeting of organisers of under-21 gay groups in London, 23 July 1975, HCA/JCGT/1/4.

46   *GN*, issue 32, gives the venue as York.

47   Scott-Presland (2015) p568.

48   *GN*, issue 32, 20 September–3 October 1973.

49   2 WLR 897.

50   Scott-Presland (2015) p370.

51   Ibid, ppxiii–xiv and 306.

52   Ibid, p307.

53   Ibid, p575.

54   *GN*, issue 54, 12 September 1974.

55   Ibid, 'Young gays campaign appeal'.

56   HCA/CHE/9/47.

57   Email from Trevor Locke to author, 22 February 2020.

58   HCA/CHE/9/47.

59   HCA/CHE/9/47.

60   Todmorden, West Yorkshire, about 45 minutes by train to Manchester, where CHE was based. Chris Bowden-Smith lived in Todmorden and it became quite a hub for young CHE activists (telephone conversation with Trevor Locke, 4 November 2020).

61   HCA/CHE/9/47.

62   HCA/CHE/8/29.

63   *The Scotsman*, 23 December 1974.

64   *Daily Mirror*, 13 September 1974, 'Rumpus over a call for Gay Lib Charter'.

65   CHE/YSIP Mailing 75/12a.

66   The two-part documentary can be viewed at the British Film Institute Mediatheque facilities. Ref 83291. The story was also captured in a book by Michael Deakin and John Willis: *Johnny Go Home* (1976: Futura Publications/Quartet Books London) ISBN 0 8600 7339 4.

67   Grey (1992) p191.

68   Deakin M and Willis J (1976), op cit, give 58 Branksome Road, Brixton, London as the centre of Gleaves' hostel empire (pp 89-90).

69   *Daily Mirror*, 23 September 1975.

70   'The Developing Role of Work in the West End', HCA/CHE/9/47.

71   Albany Trust files HCA/Albany Trust/16/2 and 16/9.

72   British Library Misc leaflets, X.0329/41. Also HCA/Albany Trust/16/61.

73   HCA/Albany Trust 16/50.

74   Mentioned at the beginning of the chapter. The first meeting held on 12 October 1975 was followed by a second meeting on 20 November

1975. Present at the second meeting (entitled 'Teenagers at Risk') were representations from Bow Street Probation Office, Friend, Gay Switchboard, Icebreakers, New Horizon, Nucleus, P.I.E., Soho Project, Scottish Minorities Group, WECVS, YSIP, youth workers and the Albany Trust. Notes of the meeting held at 31 Clapham Road, London SW9, are in LSE HCA/CHE2/12/39 (a partially open file examined by the author 8 October 2018).

75 Later Sir Harold Haywood, CEO of the National Association of Youth Clubs and subsequently the Prince's Trust.

76 See Earl's Court Project meeting, 19 May 1977; 'Chris Heaume to monitor the work being done by the CYSA (Community and Youth Service Association)', HCA/Albany Trust/16/19. Also 'Proposed Youth Centre for Young Homosexuals in Earl's Court: Advice' four-page document produced by lawyer based at 2 Pump Court, Temple, London EC 4. 9 September 1977 (signature looks like Jones). Document in Legal Position of LGTG file (London Gay Teenage Group, B20/050 (uncat) London Metropolitan Archives/City of London).

77 HCA/Albany Trust 16/50.

78 Chris Heaume email to author, 26 August 2020.

79 The term 'Young Gays Campaign' was still being used despite the committee recommending in December 1974 to the executive of CHE that the title be changed from the 'Young Gays Campaign' to the 'CHE Youth Services Information Project' (YSIP).

80 GN issue 64, 13–26 February 1975, 'Procuring reform'.

81 HCA/CHE/9/47.

82 Letter Trevor Locke to Pat O'Connor, 2 July 1975, HCA/CHE/7/14/A.

83 HCA/CHE/7/14/A.

84 YLG Newsletter, mid-September–early October 1976, HCA/CHE/7/14/A.

85 Paul Welch came from Surbiton, Surrey.

86 HCA/JCGT/1/4.

87 HCA/CHE/7/14/A .

88 HCA/JCGT/1/4 minute 9. The minute also states the executive committee of CHE would be asked to accept three recommendations: 1. That CHE should set up a group specifically for under-21s in London and that it would seek recognition at the December national council. 2. That CHE should recommend to the present youth group that it should change its name when the teenage group is set up. 3. That

YSIP should publish a leaflet giving details about operating under-21s groups.

89   CHE LIC was right in the sex industry part of Soho. 'A dingy backstreet tucked off Piccadilly Circus' next to strippers in the Windmill Theatre. Scott-Presland (2015) pp406–7.

90   *GN* issue 78, 1975.

91   HCA/CHE/8/10 papers for 22–25 August 1975, CHE Conference, and *GN* issue 78.

92   'How did the pro-paedophile group PIE exist openly for 10 years?' Tom de Castella and Tom Heyden, *BBC News Magazine*, 27 February 2014, https://www.bbc.co.uk/news/magazine-26352378 (accessed 4 July 2021).

93   'Allegations of child sexual abuse linked to Westminster' (2020). A report of the inquiry panel; Professor Alexis Jay OBE, Professor Sir Malcolm Evans KCMG OBE, Ivor Frank, Drusilla Sharpling CBE, as part of the Independent Inquiry into Child Sexual Abuse.

94   Trevor Locke, 'The Future of Y.S.I.P. – an opinion', unpublished paper dated 4 September 1975 (copy kindly lent to me by Trevor Locke).

95   *GN* issue 79, 1975. Tel Airs was publicity officer for Milton Keynes CHE in February 1975, *GN* issue 64, 13–26 February 1975.

96   *GN* issue 81, 23 October–5 November 1975.

97   Originally called the Young Gays Campaign.

98   CHE Annual Report 1975.

99   HCA/CHE/2/5.

100   Report by Tel Airs in CHE Annual Report 1976.

101   *GN* issue 93, 22 April 1976. The Home Secretary at the time was Roy Jenkins and he had no appetite for further reform so soon after the 1967 Act.

102   CHE *Youth News* vol 1, December/January. HCA/CHE/4/8.

103   *GN* issue 93, 22 April 1976.

104   22 May 1976, CHE Minutes Executive Committee Report on CHE Teenage Movement 76/079 – source Trevor Locke.

105   22 May 1976, CHE Minutes Executive Committee Report on CHE Teenage Movement 76/079 – source Trevor Locke.

106   *Offensive Prose.* The author has not been able to locate a copy of this book in any library or archive.

107   Gary James was seeing the others off. He did not attend the conference (telephone conversation with author, 23 September 2020). Gary James

(born 1958), from Tunbridge Wells, was a good friend of Philip Cox. On 'Gaywaves' radio Gary appeared as Gary Mewis (Gaywaves broadcast 19 January 1983, BL C586/525 s1). Gary James published *Spangles, Glam, Gaywaves and Tubes* in 2019 (Book Guild Publishing Ltd). He dedicated the book to Phil Cox. Gary James was a founding member of the Young People's Theatre Scheme at the Royal Court Theatre. He was also a member of the political touring theatre company Gay Sweatshop. In an email to the author (17 September 2020), Gary states that he cannot recall ever personally attending any LGTG meetings at Friend or the Oval, and that he never attended at 296 Holloway Road. 'I don't recall ever going to a Friend meeting and I certainly never went to Holloway Road. I do recall having a conversation with Phil about attending Teenage Group meetings once we had turned 20. I was very strict with myself about that and refused to go to anything when I wasn't actually a teenager any more. That would have been any time after I turned 20 in June 1978.'

108   *Metro* no 7, 29 October 1978. See also Andrew Martin's report 'A Club with No Leader' (no date but possibly typed up 1979), where he mentions meetings held in London Friend's back room in Islington. They were mainly discussing how to get proper premises and funding, coffee and biscuits. Andrew Martin states that these meetings at Friend were *before* meetings at the Oval. Steve Power has stated that the meetings at the Oval were *before* meetings at London Friend, where the nucleus of the early LGTG combined with some young people who were meeting at London Friend.

109   James op cit. pp 56–57 (2019). Gary James telephone conversation with author, 23 September 2020. James told me that both Philip Cox and Paul Welch, who started the Gay Teenage Group, were in a relationship, living in at 99 Godfrey House, Bath Street, and working at the GLC. When Gary first met them they were splitting up.

110   Chris Heaume email to author, 1 February 2020. And a further email of 9 September 2020 to explain how 'far from the cafe' could mean just a short distance: '5 metres, through a corridor from the main building. Remember, when people timidly sought us out then, they didn't want anyone else to see when or know why they were there. We weren't in any way visible in an annexe. And to put up signs in the public cafe saying "gay Teenagers here" felt too public'.

111   CHE *Youth News* issue 4, 1976, p10. Steve Power states that the group

that met at London Friend included Philip Cox, Gary James and Paul Welch. They were the original core of what became the LGTG (email 1 February 2020). Gary states he never went to meetings at London Friend (see footnote 107).

112   Steve Power, message to author on Facebook, 13 September 2020.

113   Scott-Presland (2015) p385.

114   HCA/Albany Trust/16/12.

115   Steve Power notes sent to author, 1 February 2019.

116   Minute 76/118f, HCA/CHE2/2/1.

117   23 October 1976, minute 76/152 h, HCA/CHE2/2/1.

118   Four years later, in 1981, Tom Haworth represented young people on the CHE executive committee.

119   Steve Power recollections of conversation with Philip Cox in late 1976 or early 1977, email to author, 10 August 2019.

120   Andrew Martin's report for the annual report: 'A club with no leader?', not dated but possibly typed up 1979.

121   Grapevine was set up as a sex education service in 1972. It provided a service in the London Boroughs of Camden and Islington and was featured on BBC 2 in their *Open Door* series in 1974. 'Judy Lamb was the part-time worker at Grapevine in Holloway Road who sat with us in the office on every Sunday' (Steve Power, email to author, 2 February 2020).

122   Steve Power notes sent to author, 1 February 2019. It took six months' training to become a recognised volunteer on Switchboard.

123   Steve Power notes sent to author, 1 February 2019. *A Bigger Splash* is a 1973 (sometimes cited as 1974) British documentary film about David Hockney's lingering breakup with his then-partner Peter Schlesinger, from 1970 to 1973. Directed by Jack Hazan and edited by David Mingay.

124   CHE *Youth News* no 5, 1976.

125   In fact Philip left the group nearly a year before he would turn 21.

126   Steve Power notes sent to author, 1 February 2019.

127   Steve Power email to author, 10 February 2020. Based on correspondence Steve Power had with Philip's sibling.

128   Recording of Gaywaves radio broadcast, 19 January 1983. BL C586/525 s 1.

129   Philip Cox featured in *Gay News* November 1977 as 'Switchboard's newest and youngest volunteer'. He was 21 at the time.

130   Andy was Andrew Martin, also known as Leo Andrew Martin and sometimes Andi.

131   Email Steve Power to author, 22 August 2019.

132   *GN* issue 112, 10–26 February 1977.

133   See Andrew Martin's LGTG draft report for 1979.

134   Steve Power notes sent to author, 1 February 2019.

135   CHE Young London Newsletter February 1981 HCA/Journal/649J.

136   Steve Power notes sent to author, 1 February 2019.

137   Bronski Beat formed in 1983 and Martin was actually corresponding with his LGTG penfriend several years earlier.

138   Sent via Steve Power to author, by message on Facebook, 9 June 2020.

139   Listed in *GN* issue 114, 10–26 March 1977.

140   Gay Switchboard logbooks held at the Bishopsgate Institute archives (closed under Data Protection Regulations).

141   Minutes of SAYS/Gay Youth Workers Group, 28 April 1977, HCA/Albany Trust/16/51.

142   *GN* issue 119, 19 May–1 June 1977. The photographs were taken at the LGTG on 17 April 1977 and are held at the Bishopsgate Institute WORKMAN/502 and WORKMAN/503.

143   HCA/Albany Trust/16/19.

144   *GN* issue 120, 2 June 1977.

145   Steve Power collection of papers. Steve states this report was produced for Grapevine after the trial period of six months in their premises, and it was produced for The Family Planning Association (Grapevine's funder) to inform their decision on whether or not to allow the LGTG to continue using the premises (email Steve Power to author 10 February 2020).

146   Steve Power notes sent to author, 1 February 2019.

147   Steve Power email to author, 26 August 2020.

148   Chris Heaume email to author, 29 August 2018.

149   Steve Power message on closed Facebook group, 15 September 2020.

150   London Weekend Television broadcast 11 episodes of *Gay Life* in 1980 (first series) and 1981 (second series), so maybe Tigger is referring to another documentary in 1977.

151   Message to author on Facebook, 29 January 2019.

152   LGTG Leaflet HCA/Albany Trust/11/40.

153   HCA/Albany Trust16/51 minutes of Sexual Awareness in Youth Services (SAYS) meeting, 10 February 1977.

154   Visit to Manchester and extensive perusal of their archives, 7 December 2019.

155   Robert named the adult who seduced him, and who had exploited his position of trust and also committed a criminal act. However, the author has not published the name. It is thought the individual left the U.K. and it is not known if they are still alive.

156   Robert Gibbs' account related to author by telephone, 5 January 2019.

157   Michael Connew to author, message on Facebook, 29 May 2020.

158   Chris Heaume email to author,11 January 2019.

159   LGTG Project Survey sheet completed by Matt Bourne. Steve Power's papers.

160   *GN* issue 143, 18–31 May.

161   Typed-up photocopied notes in Steve Power's papers.

162   Inner Local Education Authority – Background to London Gay Teenage Group. Application for recognition by ILEA Youth Service. Paper by Randal Davies, Islington Youth Officer, White Lion Street, London N1, 15 May 1978. Steve Power's papers.

163   On 8 November 2020 the footage was made available to all on YouTube: LGTG_VTS_01_1https://www.youtube.com/watch?v=No1fIjUUQ0s (accessed 4 July 2021).

164   Email Martin Collins to the author, 10 May 2018.

165   Robert Ian Halls' death certificate gives his address, and place of death, as 12 Talbot Road, Carshalton. His cause of death is bronchopneumonia.

166   Letter dated 16 May 1978 in Steve Power's papers.

167   *GN*, 15 June 1978, 'It's not all Rose's'.

168   From LGTG INFO 78 bulletin. Steve Power's papers.

169   ILEA CEC.1 54/78. The report states that: 'In addition to the application for registration received by the Islington Area Youth Committee, the Kensington and Chelsea Area Youth Committee has discussed the work of the "SW5" Group which also seeks to make provision for young homosexuals'. London SW5 is the Earl's Court area and 'SW5' may have been the name for the Earl's Court Project referred to earlier. Copy given to author by Chris Heaume.

170   Additional sheet on 'Registration of groups dealing with young homosexuals: Observations of the Medical Adviser [sic] on a letter from the Nationwide Festival of Light'. Undated. There is also a page of typed notes on homosexuality dated 3 July 1978 with reference MA/Sec/GSW. These two pages were thought to accompany the report CEC.1 54/78 referred to above. Copies of both pages given by Chris Heaume to author.

171   Ibid.

172   Dr Fay Hutchinson born 1 December 1926, died 5 June 2009. She was a founder member of the Institute of Psychosexual Medicine in 1974 and a pioneer in the field of sexual health. Obituary in *Journal of Family Planning and Reproductive Health Care* 35(4):264, October 2009.

173   Chris Heaume email, 31 January 2020. Also typed-up document: 'Adolescent sexuality and implications on work of the Area Youth Committee. Notes on talk by Dr Fay Hutchingson [*sic*] at the A.Y.C. of 22.3.78'. This document may have been presented to the London Youth Committee. It is not known who typed up the notes of the talk given to the area youth committee on 22 March 1978. Copy of document provided to author by Chris Heaume.

174   Author's recollection in an interview with Martha Rhodes Robinson, in 2018, as part of her research on bisexuals (for a PhD at the University of Birmingham).

175   Claire Lawrie's first film, *Beyond 'There's always a black issue Dear' 2018* (2019).

176   Held 7–9 July 1978 at Earnshaw Hall, Sheffield University.

177   Steve Power message to author on Facebook, 30 January 2020.

178   Steve Power message to author on Facebook, 30 January 2020.

179   *The Guardian*, 28 September 1978.

180   HC/Ephemera/347. The three gay teenage groups were believed to be the LGTG, Leicester Gay Teenage Group and Merseyside Gay Youth Group (all founder members of the JCGT in January 1979). Merseyside Gay Youth Group were listed in advertising as early as 1977 in the *Liverpool Echo*, 29 March 1977.

181   Micky Burbidge papers HCA/JCGT/1/3.

182   The JCGT's papers are held at the London School of Economics in the Hall-Carpenter Archives.

183   HCA/CHE2/2/1.

184   LGBTM/228.

185   HCA/CHE2/2/1 information sheet of February 1976, 'CHE Education Kit Special Announcement'.

186   LGTG results of meeting, Friday 22 September 1978. Two-page typed-up notes given to the author by Matthew Scudamore (LMA London Gay Teenage Group, B20/050 (uncat)). LGTG Minutes of meeting, 27 October 1978, reports 'The possibility of us using a room at the "Play Space for Children" has fallen through' (Steve Power's papers).

187   *GN*, 16 November 1978.

188   *The London Glue Teenache Grope [sic] magazine substitute* by Leo Andrew Martin, not dated [but 1978], which includes the agenda [actually notes of the meeting which had been held] for the meeting at the Kentish Town Project, 4 Caversham Road on Friday 1 December 1978. This three page 'newsletter' also mentions a football team being formed and consisting of Andrew Martin, Keiron Reynolds, Cliff Williams [author], Peter Langford and Steve Power (Steve Power's papers). As far as the author is aware the football never happened.

189   'Special message for two social workers, a computer designer, a member of the Gay Activist Alliance and five members of the London Gay Teenage Group' by Andrew Martin in *The London Glue Teenache Grope [sic] magazine substitute,* no date [1978].

190   When the Tom Robinson Band reached number 18 in the charts in 1978 with 'Glad to Be Gay' the BBC refused to play it on their chart show. It was first performed on television on 24 July 1977, being introduced by Janet Street Porter on *The London Weekend Show* (*From the Vaults* by Gary Garvey, Sky Arts Channel, 2 October 2020).

191   Author's recollection in an interview with Martha Rhodes Robinson in 2018, as part of her research on bisexuals (for a PhD at the University of Birmingham). Steve Power has a tape cassette labelled 'LGTG Radio London Interview' 3 (?-difficult to read exact date) December 1978. This tape cassette may be a recording of the Malcolm Laycock radio broadcast the author refers to.

192   Michael Connew comment on closed Facebook group, 31 January 2019.

193   *The Observer*, 7 January 1979.

194   LGTG Info '79, results of meeting, 2 February 1979. Steve Power's papers.

195   Ibid. 2 February 1979. Steve Power's papers.

196   Letter (two pages), Micky Burbidge to Steve Power, 8 February 1979. Steve Power's papers.

197   *Daily Telegraph*, 2 February 1979; see also *GN* issue 161, 22 February–7 March 1979, which reported that NABC official Barry Walsh said he had visited the London Gay Teenage Group and was very impressed with the work they did but did not support separate clubs for young gay people. The NABC thought they should be welcome into their clubs.

198   Collective meeting, 2 March 1979. Steve Power's papers. Manor Gardens, off Holloway Road, now a welfare trust, originally opened in 1913.

199   *Breaking the Silence*, 1981, p43.

200   Nationwide Festival of Light Bulletin, issue 5. Steve Power's papers. Steve's copy has the following written note on it. 'Andrew Martin reported back a conversation between him and Rose Robertson. Rose had shown him a letter between Margaret Thatcher and Mary Whitehouse. Mary was seeking support to prosecute LGTG members (committee). Micky Burbidge looked into it further and the letter seems like they are going for PIE. Upon further discussion we learnt that Dennis [sic] Lemon, Editor of Gay News, was being prosecuted. It was inevitable that we were next. Legal support was required and a Law Lords ruling sought'.

201   Just north of Beacon Hill, near Grayshott. Now a privately-owned adventure camp. The site was at the time run by ILEA. Shelia was the only female in the party of 12 young people. When the group, who were the only ones camping there, used the site swimming pool they were reported by the caretaker for bathing nude! (Author's recollection.) The group had spent a weekend at the same site in 1978 (18–21 August) but it is not known how many attended then.

202   Possibly Ralph's disco held in the cellar of a large private house in Farnham. Conversation at LSE with Philip Ingesant, 7 August 2019.

203   'The Liberal Party: The Real Fight is for Britain, Election Manifesto'. Under the heading of 'Minority Rights' the manifesto calls for 'Removing all legal discrimination based on sexual orientation'. David Steel led the party after Jeremy Thorpe had resigned in 1976. Amazingly Thorpe stood in his parliamentary seat of North Devon at the 1979 general election. At the time he was awaiting trial for conspiracy to murder charges. This all arose from a gay affair he had wanted to keep quiet.

204   Reprinted in LGTG Annual Report 1982.

205   LGTG INFO 79. Item in Steve Power's papers.

206   Letter Brian Earl to Chris Heaume, 30 April 1979.

207   Letter Brian Earl to Steve Power, 10 May 1979. See also Manor Gardens LMA/4314/01/02, North Islington Welfare Executive Committee meetings, 3 April 1979, minute 8i.

208   The London Gay Teenage Group, leaflet dated June 1979. Produced by Andrew Martin. Islington Local History Centre collection S/IP/1/1/3/2.

209   Anal intercourse can potentially weaken the anal sphincter muscle and so if someone is on the receiving end a lot this can cause incontinence

in some bowels. The point that was being raised rather assumed homosexual sex was always anal sex.

210   Steve Power comment on closed Facebook group, 25 September 2020.

211   'Gay youth clubs get official OK' *GN* 28 June–11 July 1979, issue 170. A one-page report of the London Youth Committee: 'Registration of Groups dealing with homosexuals' (undated) summarises the debate about the registration of homosexual youth groups. 'A proposal was put to the Committee "that this Committee supports the removal of the embargo on the registration of homosexual youth groups". The voting was For 12, Against 4, Abstentions 4.' Handwritten note by Steve Power at top of the page '1979 London Youth Committee Outcome and Vote'. Steve Power's papers.

212   Chris Heaume email to author, 6 January 2019.

213   BBC *Radio Times* issue 2,902, and letter, John Sketchley to Robert Longley, 18 June 1979. HCA/JCGT/3/4.

214   Letter, 23 August 1979, from Chris Heaume to members of the management committee. Sent with papers (agenda and draft constitution) for committee meeting at Manor Gardens, 4 September 1979 at 7.30pm. Report of the meeting in *Metro, Magazine of the London Gay Teenage Group* issue 13. Steve Power's papers.

215   Named after Geraldine Maitland Aves D.B.E. (1898–1986).

216   *Metro* issue 14, 1979. Steve Power's papers.

217   ILEA/PS/AY005/04/1. In Green File: Minutes of LGTG Management Committee, 26 September 1979, attended by Fay Hutchinson (Brook Advisory Service), Jane Dixon (Camden Girls Project), Brian Travers (Westminster Detached Project), Steven Power (Grapevine), Alun Williams (Grapevine), Gerard Hendra (London Friend), Brian Earl (Manor Gardens Welfare Centre), Andrew Martin (Elisabeth House and LGTG), Mary, Tracy and Philip (three LGTG members). The Green File also contains correspondence regarding applying for funding for a part-time youth worker for the group, e.g. Steve Power to John Stott (Islington Area Youth Officer) 23 February 1980.

218   Leaflet in Islington Local History Centre collection.

219   *Daily Mirror*, 25 May 1979 p21.

220   Draft versions in HCA/Albany Trust/16/24. I have not been able to find the final version.

221   Martin Collins email to author, 5 November 2019.

222   *GN* issue 176, 4 October–17 October 1979.

223 JCGT Survey of Callers to Help Organisations. Annex to Initial Report. MB June 1979 HCA/JCGT/1/1.

224 CHE executive committee minute 79/95, 16 June 1979 HCA/CHE 2/2/1.

225 *Daily Telegraph*, 27 November 1979, 'Way of the World' column by Peter Simple. LAGNA.

226 Letter, 30 November 1979, A Grey to W F Deedes. LAGNA.

227 Thomas Flanagan, E-communication on private Facebook group, 18 July 2019. The NAYC conference was at Hull in 1980.

228 Minutes of JCGT meeting Liverpool, 1 December 1979, HCA/JCGT/1/3.

229 The police were watching the gay bar at closing time and pounced on the young man who was writing the word 'plague' with a marker pen on the outside of the building as the group left. He was swiftly arrested and taken in a police van to the nearby Victorian cell block where he spent a few hours before being charged with criminal damage and bailed. An appearance at Dale Street Magistrates' Court followed on Monday and a £50 fine. The fine was paid by Micky Burbidge. Liverpool's old Main Bridewell in Cheapside, where the young culprit was taken, is still standing, although it now is student and visitor accommodation. It was first opened in 1867, having been built in the Victorian tradition of striking fear into anyone who had to spend some time there under lock and key. It had approximately 60 cells with each having a heavy wood door and many of the cells measuring just seven foot by seven foot in total accommodation size. In 1981 another young gay man claimed he was raped by a police officers in a cell there (' "Riot police raped me" claims Liverpool Kevin' *Capital Gay*, 28 August 1981 p16).

230 The cost was just £4 each plus a share of the petrol for the minibus. *Metro: Magazine of the London Gay Teenage Group*, issue 18. Steve Power's papers.

231 *GN*, issue 183 24 January 1980, meeting Monday evenings at Manor Gardens.

232 CHE broadsheet, March 1980, HCA/CHE/7/114.

233 Greg told me, in the summer of 1979, that he had been the election agent for the Labour candidate in the East Surrey constituency during the 1979 General Election. He must have been one of the youngest election agents for a major party.

234 The British Library hold copies of *Mister Magazine*. Readers wishing to view them are supervised in the Rare Books (special materials) Room

at St Pancras. Volume 3 , number 2 was published in 1980 and sold for £2.50.

235   *GN,* issue 95, in May 1976, stated that Icebreakers have 'recently taken over the regular disco at the Prince Albert, Wharfedale Road, N.1. Fri 8.30pm Adm 25p' . This was the first gay disco the author attended in late 1978 or early 1979.

236   BL C586/319 S2 C2.

237   *Capital Gay,* 11 March 1983.

238   Kevin O'Neill recollection on closed Facebook group, 15 September 2020.

239   LMA/ILEA/PS/AY005/04/1 in the Green File contains the applications for grants from ILEA and details of who applied from the LGTG to attend the Hull conference: David Irving, Roy Puddefoot, Keiron Brennan, Maureen Hand, Cliff Wylie, Neville Magee, Glen Perry, Thomas Flanagan, John Barry, C Jones. All of these, except Thomas Flanagan, were eligible for a grant of 50% of the cost of attending. Thomas lived outside ILEA so was not eligible (letter T H Stacey, ILEA, to A Williams, LGTG, 17 July 1980). There are five other application forms for this conference on file which may have been settled later (A Miller, Jo Ritchie, H S McCormack, D A Lowe, G(loria) Simpson). The author lived outside the ILEA area but applied to attend as Cliff Wylie and gave his friend's address at 51 Huntingdon Street, N1! It was a special surprise for the author to discover this document 40 years later in the archives. And here I can set the record straight! How many more aliases were used in surviving documents relating to the LGTG?

240   Minutes of LGTG management committee, 23 June 1980, LMA/ILEA/PS/AY005/04/01.

241   The group was continuing to apply for funded part-time youth worker hours. This was at a time when Islington Youth Office was having to make some cuts to expenditure. Papers in LMA/ILEA/PS/AY005/04/01 include a letter from the Kentish Town Project to Islington (23 January 1981) stating what 'an extremely important resource for young people in London' the group was and supporting them in their request for more funds. Notes follow to explain how the group was supported by Islington (Borough Council) and how it ran well on a voluntary basis. A one-off grant of £450 was paid to the group (to tide them over difficult times) by Islington AYO as

acknowledged by Martin Collins (treasurer, LGTG) in a letter, 11 December 1981, to the Islington AYO.

242 Martin Collins email to author, 25 October 2020.

243 Jain Clarke was a 'Jane Clarke' but altered the spelling of her first name to distinguish herself from another Jane Clarke who was also involved in the JCGT. Both Jane Clarkes attended the lobby of Parliament on 7 July 1980.

244 *GN*, issue 196, 24 July 1980. HCA/JCGT/1/1 contains minutes and agendas of JCGT meetings, as well as papers on the Parliamentary lobby.

245 *GN*, issue 192, 29 May 1980.

246 'Birth of GYM', *GN*, issue 197, 21 August 1980.

247 *Birmingham Post*, 10 July 1980.

248 *Daily Telegraph*, 11 July 1980.

249 HCA/JCGT/1/3.

250 Claire Rayner, *Sunday Mirror*, 30 November 1980.

251 An earlier East London GLF, with an address of 103 Market, London E6, meeting on Thursdays, was listed in 1972–73 in *Leeds Broadsheet* no 13, January 1973 (HCA/Journals/280D).

252 *Peace News*, 23 January 1981, mentions *Pink Gym* 'well produced for a duplicated format' at 45 pence, being produced by the GYM and available from the LGTG in Manor Gardens. Number 1 was October 1980 and sold for 45p (Martin Collins collection).

253 The sponsorship scheme is mentioned in *GN* issue 215, 14 May 1981. Ten pounds would sponsor a week of the group.

254 Martin Collins email to author, 5 November 2019.

255 Gregg Blachford's papers in Hall Carpenter Archives.

256 LGTG- A member's perspective: an open letter to members of the LGTG by Jay McLaren, Kevin O'Neill and Gary Barker, April 1981. Gregg Blachford's papers in Hall Carpenter Archives.

257 HCA/JCGT/1/3 leaflet, 30–31 May 1981.

258 Richard Desmond comment on closed Facebook group, 7 June 2020. Robert Webber was 18 on 10 June 1982. He died in April 1992.

259 Richard Desmond left Gay Switchboard at Lisa Power's request when he was 16. Lisa describes how he was rather excitable and noisy and how difficult it was working the Switchboard in a very small room. Richard returned older and wiser in 1993. The tale is related in Episode 8 of *The Log Books: stories from Britain's LGBT+ history and conversations about*

being queer today, produced by Shivani Dave, Tash Walker and Adam Zmith, in partnership with Switchboard, the LGBT+ helpline (podcast available online).

260   Ash Kotak email to author, 9 March 2020.

261   Gavin Simmons to author, message on Facebook 31 May 2019.

262   *Just Seventeen*, 26 June 1985.

263   Feather (2015) p387. Copies of *Gay Youth*, issues 1–9 (June 1981–June 1983), are held in the British Library. Some later copies are in the HCA. The last known edition is number 21 in 1987.

264   LMA/ILEA/PS/AY005/04/01 including a letter from Brent Council Social Services Department to Islington Youth Service (4 March 1981) concerning a 14-year-old boy from Brent in care of the local authority who was 'attending a gay club in your area' (presumably the LGTG). There were also complaints from a parent about their 15-year-old son attending the LGTG and him being indecently assaulted by members and a youth worker. A letter from Winston Pinder (Islington Youth Service) to Gary Barker (LGTG) followed (2 April 1981), pointing out that this complaint was of 'serious concern'. It is believed the parents of the boy took the matter to the police but it is not known if anything resulted from the allegations. The issue of under-16-year-olds at the LGTG was taken up again by Ray Walker (Islington Youth Service) to Tom Haworth (LGTG) in a letter of 21 January 1982. Walker points out that if the LGTG fail to comply with the guidelines and age limits 'I would have no alternative but to withdraw registration, and with it any resources which the Area Youth Committee have agreed'.

265   Letter Vincent Knight-Newbury to Micky Burbidge, 10 October 1979, HCA/JCGT/3/5.

266   JCGT minutes of meeting, 7 March 1981, HCA/JCGT/1/3. In Manchester about 15 attend each Thursday. Steve Power was developing a group in Bradford. The Stoke Youth Group collapsed and merged with the men's group. By August the Tyneside Gay Teenage Group was in existence. They ran a session at the Durham GayFest and also at the second JCGT Weekend Workshop in Liverpool 21–22 November 1981. HCA/JCGT/3/5.

267   On 19 June 1984 four representatives of this group held a discussion with 6th-form pupils at Walworth Secondary Comprehensive School. A full report on this event was produced by Keith Trotman (ex-pupil) and others. Keith Trotman was a young Black gay man who later worked

at the Greenwich Lesbian and Gay Centre. Not to be confused with another Keith Trotman, a young white man, who was in the Gay Youth Movement and who is mentioned by Jon Pyper in Chapter 13.

268   *Capital Gay*, 7 August 1981.

269   *Gay Youth*, autumn issue 3, 1981.

270   *Gay Youth*, issue 7, October/November 1982.

271   *Capital Gay*, 11 September 1981.

272   Jain Clarke was a 'Jane Clarke' but altered the spelling of her first name to distinguish herself from another Jane Clarke who was involved in the JCGT.

273   LGTG, 9 September 1981 and 9 November 1981 minutes of management committee, HCA/Ephemera/347.

274   Letter Steve Power to Islington Area Youth Committee, 5 October 1979, stating the amended constitution. Previous wording on age had been 'Membership of the group shall be open to young people between the ages of 16 and 21 years old, inclusive, whether they be homosexual, heterosexual or bisexual'. The amendment, required by the AYC, was dropping the word 'inclusive' so as to make clear the cut-off for members was on reaching 21, not 22, years of age, LMA/ILEA/PS/AY005/04/01.

275   Minutes of LGTG management committee, 5 October 1981. Matthew Scudamore's papers (deposited in the LMA: London Gay Teenage Group, B20/050 (uncat)).

276   *Kicks* issue 1, 1 November 1981.

277   *Gay Youth* issue 3, autumn 1981.

278   HCA/JCGT/1/2. Coppull, Lancashire, is a village of about 8,000 so it is surprising it had set up a gay youth group. I have not been able to ascertain how long it lasted and how many young people ever went along.

279   Maureen Hand conversation, 14 February 2020.

280   *Islington Gazette*, 5 February 1982.

281   Letter O R Johnston, Director of the Nationwide Festival of Light, to Peter Newsam Director of the ILEA, 26 January 1982, LMA/ILEA/PS/AY005/04/01.

282   Youth Clubs (Homosexuals), House of Commons debate, 1 February 1982, vol 17 c33W, https://api.parliament.uk/historic-hansard/written-answers/1982/feb/01/youth-clubs-homosexuals#S6CV0017P0_19820201_CWA_224 (accessed 4 July 2021).

283 'Youth Chief Backs Cash for Teenage...', *Islington Gazette*, 5 February 1982, Islington Local History Centre, S/IP/1/1/3/8.

284 *Surrey Comet and South Middlesex News*, 27 February 1982.

285 *GN* issue 236, 18–31 March 1982, 'Manchester: The Muck and the Magic'.

286 There had been some elements of 'social education' and political awareness organised by the group previously. For example, from January–April 1980 the group ran a seven-week course for 20 young people examining the roles played in relationships, sexual and emotional relationships and the lesbian experience. LMA/ILEA/PS/AY005/04/01 contains the application for funding for this course of £130 to pay for hire of films and a production by Gay Sweatshop to be performed at one session.

287 Gregg Blachford (born Toronto 1950), lived in Canada from 1950–71, Australia from 1971–73, UK from 1973–79, Germany from 1979–81, UK from 1981–1990 and then back to Canada. He was a masters student at Essex in 1977, supervised by Ken Plummer.

288 Museum of Youth Culture interview 11 March 2021, https://museumofyouthculture.com/eleanor-affleck/?fbclid=IwAR10YGc9KjEqo2tJk-910oUIIb4g2_eqOI8TDhvEuQP9Lw5rVi9n6cAJoFA (accessed 4 July 2021).

289 *GN* issue 245, 22 July–4 August 1982. Owen originally came from South Africa.

290 Television broadcast *The London Programme*, 15 April 1983, https://www.youtube.com/watch?v=RRWvcdyQITs (accessed 4 July 2021).

291 As previously described it was actually at the end of 1976 that the group started meeting at Grapevine in Holloway Road, and the 'official launch' was February 1977 not 1976.

292 George Tremlett, GLC Councillor.

293 Draft constitution. London Gay Teenage Group. Four-page typed document in Matthew Scudamore's collection of papers (deposited in the LMA: London Gay Teenage Group, B20/050 [uncat]).

294 One person stated to the author that he first attended the LGTG aged 23. He looked a lot younger and was assumed to be under 21. He 'confessed' to two other members that he was in fact 23. The decision was made to put him on the management committee where he served usefully for a few years. The author has found other examples of persons first attending the LGTG aged 21 or over, but pretending to be under 21.

295   LGTG Annual Report, 1982, p25.

296   Minutes of the LGTG management committee, 8 December 1982, show additional management committee members: Christopher Lloyd (secretary), Sarah Wilkinson, Paul Williams (Gay Switchboard presumably replacing Mark Ashton), Robert Lang (Icebreakers), Vincent Knight (also known as Knight-Newbury) and Gus Cairns. Treasurer Martin Collins and youth worker Gregg Blachford were also on the committee at the time.

297   *GN* issue 238, 15–28 April 1982.

298   *Capital Gay*, 28 May 1982. See also *GN* issues 244 and 245 on the age of consent debate. In issue 245, Martin Higgins, from Oxford, states that he attended the GYM committee on 27 June where a 'no age of consent' was discussed. Higgins expressed his discontent and urged others to do so: 'To equate child sexuality with adult sexuality is both foolish and dangerous.'

299   HCA/McLellan/10.

300   British Library, C586/343 and C586/309 S1 C2.

301   Marc E Burke (1993) *Coming Out of the Blue*. Marc informed the part-time youth worker that he was in the police but was anxious that no-one else in the group knew. After a while the information filtered through to attenders. How did that happen? When Marc went to gay venues, like Heaven, he was careful to avoid being seen by any police officer. He was scared he would be recognised. Marc stated to the author that he was actually over the 21 age limit of the group when he first attended and that he either lied about his age or they overlooked it when they knew he was too old for the group (e-communication with author, October 2020).

302   Marc Burke email to author, 27 October 2020. The bit about jumping off the M25 overpasses was 'meant to be slightly tongue in cheek. I would never have jumped off a bridge when there were perfectly good, old fashioned razor blades in the house in those days' (email to author, 29 October 2020). The building of the M25 section from Godstone to Reigate (junctions 6 to 8) was first planned in 1966 and opened in February 1976.

303   The group was meeting on Monday nights in Catford for 16- to 21-year-olds. *Capital Gay*, 3 September 1982.

304   Copies of *Jeune* are held at the LSE HCA/Ephemera/432. Issue 1 is dated November/December 1981. The Southampton group met on

Sunday afternoons at the Unemployment Advice Centre (Old Slipper Baths), Portchester Road.

305   *Capital Gay*, 17 September 1982.

306   *Capital Gay*, 24 September 1982.

307   *Capital Gay*, 1 October 1982. The article on the jumble sale also states the LGTG has a new telephone number, 01-272-5741.

308   E-communication, 3 March 2019 from Jane Clarke, who was chair of the LGTG at the time.

309   *The Mancunian Gay* issue 16, November 1982 (Manchester City Archives).

310   https://player.bfi.org.uk/free/film/watch-true-romance-etc-1982-online BFI website (accessed 4 July 2021).

311   *HIM Monthly* issue 51, October 1982, pp49–50 and p55.

312   One-page notice of event sent by Simon Bulpin, LGTG Secretary. The cottage was rented from the Inter-Action Advisory Service. Steve Lunniss's papers.

313   *Capital Gay*, 26 November 1982. Steve Power recalled 'a party at Robert's flat. An American guy called Tilo [Rechenbach], a friend of one of the members had arrived from New York. He was young and handsome but the talk away from him at the party, was of him likely having AIDS, because he was American. Folk were seriously stereotyping. It shook me at the time, but it was a real fear. During the party Tilo asked if I would like to spend the night with him! I thought about the conversations at the Terrence Higgins Trust (set up in 1982) and I realised that I could stay safe but it was all new. At the end of that party I did stay with Tilo and learnt that I could stay safe. He was a young gentleman who took responsibility too. We also had a number of rent boys who came to LGTG and they were fully aware of the risks. Some choosing to use protection but at the right price they would risk themselves. I found it difficult so others most certainly did. Many of us at first when HTVL3 started, didn't want to believe it, we thought it's just lies to stop us. It was a huge blow to many, it also scared some folk into not having sex at all'. Steve Power comment on closed Facebook group, 14 May 2020.

314   Clews (2017) states that the acronym AIDS was first used in USA in July 1982. Before that it had been known as GRID (Gay-Related Immune Deficiency) and before the acronym GRID, PCP. The first person to be documented as dying of the illness in the UK had been in the latter half of 1981 when it was known as PCP (pneumocystis carinii pneumonia).

315 The group met at Camden Town Hall, 12 April 1983, and subsequent meetings were held to develop policy and practical action. Steve Power's papers.

316 *Capital Gay*, 4 February 1983.

317 According to *Capital Gay* 60 people applied for the two half-time jobs at the LGTG. The wages and office in Camden were funded by a £12,000 GLC grant. *Capital Gay*, 28 January 1983 and 25 February 1983.

318 Lorraine Trenchard message on Facebook to author, 11 December 2018.

319 *Capital Gay*, 25 February 1983.

320 The Islington Bus Co. started in 1972 as a charity funded through the council and ILEA to help local groups. It came to support c. 300 groups, giving regular help with matters such as printing, and in 1976–77 moved to Palmer Place. The organisation ran a brightly painted double-decker bus that was used during weekdays as a playschool and could be booked in the evenings by any Islington group for transport or for a meeting, crèche or exhibition. Toys and equipment were also provided on loan.

321 This badge is in the HCA Collection.

322 This later proved to be an unfortunate play on words with the television programme *Jim'll Fix It*. In the TV programme Jimmy Savile fixed things for people. Subsequent to Savile's death in 2011, a long catalogue of sexual abuse by him emerged.

323 *Gay Youth* issue 7, October/November 1982.

324 Papers of The Homo Thespians 1983 in Steve Lunniss's papers. Included are details of a camping trip to the New Forest, Thursday 18 August to Monday 22 August 1983, which was attended by four people.

325 Jon is named 'Greyum' in Richard Coles's book *Fathomless Riches* (2014). Jon was previously called Graham Pyper.

326 Jon Pyper comment on closed Facebook group, 25 July 2019.

327 *Capital Gay*, 8 July 1983.

328 Hansard HC Deb, 1 July 1983, vol 44, cc804–25.

329 The same mother and son that featured in *Gay News* issue 236, and referred to in Chapter Nine. The age Kevin came out to his mother differs in this article.

330 E-correspondence to author, 20 May 2020 and 25 October 2020.

331 *Newcastle Evening Chronicle*, 16 February 1983.

332 *Newcastle Evening Chronicle*, 'Gay Group chief defends grant', 22 March, and 'Grant for gay youth group', 7 April 1986.

333 The film is available on YouTube on the London Community Video Archive pages. The Gay Youth Video Project started in the spring of 1982 – see *Capital Gay*, 1 October 1982 – a promotional film by the project made in 1982 contained film of the GYM Summer Camp self-defence course set to disco music. A flyer for what was called the Gay Teenagers Video Project advertises an event starting on Sunday 13 June 1982 at the Oval House, 54 Kennington Oval, London, to which teenagers are invited to take part to make a video film. The organisers are listed as 'Kieth [*sic*], Sarah [Perry] and Andy [Lipman]' (HCA/Ephemera/457). The Gay Teenagers Video Project could be the original name for the Lesbian and Gay Youth Video Project.

334 Weeks (2016) p244–5.

335 Lyn Thomas e-communication including Facebook, 14 August 2019.

336 *Evening Standard*, 23 December 1983.

337 Lorraine Trenchard message on Facebook to author, 26 August 2020.

338 *Capital Gay*, 17 February 1984.

339 'GYM receives about 75 letters a week from young lesbians and gay men between the ages of 12 and 26', letter Tom Midgley to Philip Conn, 7 February 1984, HCA/Friend/Additional/2/3 correspondence 1984.

340 *Something to tell you*, p145.

341 The London Apprentice.

342 Josef Cabey to author, document sent by Facebook message, 7 November 2019.

343 Steve Lunniss comment in private Facebook group, 1 January 2019.

344 Steve Lunniss comment in private message on Facebook, 20 September 2020.

345 *Capital Gay*, 6 April 1984.

346 *Gay Youth* issue 11, 1984.

347 *Lesbian and Gay Youth* magazine issue 14, January 1985.

348 *Capital Gay*, 6 April 1984.

349 Essex Gay Youth Helpline news sheet, April 1984. Steve Lunniss's papers in Islington Local History Centre.

350 Gregg Blachford in *HIM*.

351 Estimated figure of over 2,000 kindly provided by Professor Sarah Rees, Newcastle University.

352 Lorraine Trenchard's report, with black-and-white photographs, is in the Bishopsgate Institute Archives, TRENCHARD/6/4.

353 Known as Jon Pyper today.

354   *TES*, 1 June 1984.

355   Steve Lunniss sent a collection of papers to the author in autumn 2020 and this letter was amongst them. It was dated 17 March but with no year. The letter and other papers have been deposited at Steve Lunniss's request in the Islington Local History Centre. The letter itself will need to be a closed or redacted document as it contains the name and address of the 18-year-old young person.

356   Bishopsgate Institute Photographs/Format/3/3/3.

357   Steve Lunniss email to author, 9 September 2020. Also reported by Steve Lunniss in LGTG Annual Report 1984 (Bishopsgate Institute).

358   LMA GLC/DG/PRB/35/45/558.

359   *Capital Gay*, 16 November 1984.

360   Court proceedings were reported in *Lesbian and Gay Youth* magazine issue 15, Summer 1985.

361   Document in Steve Power's papers.

362   The name change did not last long. It was back to the LGTG within a year.

363   Previous LGTG zines included *Metro* (produced regularly circa 1978-80 largely by Andrew Martin), and *The SNU*. *The SNU* might have been a one off, appearing in 1985. A copy is in the Gregg Blachford papers in the LSE HCA. Steve Power has quite a few issues of *Metro*.

364   *Visions*, HCA/Ephemera/457. The author has seen six different editions of *Visions* in both the HCA and among the papers of Steve Lunniss (the latter now in the Islington Local History Centre archives). The known editions are: August '85, September '85, October '85, November '85, December '85 and January '86.

365   Gregg Blachford e-mail to author, 27 May 2020. Notes from his diary entries: Sun 5 May 1985 'First session with Kim Nagle'.

366   Islington Area Youth Office newsletter issue 12, June 1985.

367   'Do gay boys just want to have fun?: Reflections on the London Gay Teenage Group 1985–89' Anthony Hillin, Senior Youth Worker (unpublished) (2020). A list of fortnightly discussions held at the LGTG in 1986 and run by Anthony can be seen in papers in HCA/Ephemera/457. The list includes 2 March 1986 'Gay Health and AIDS', 11 May 'Racism', 22 June 'Alcoholism and Drugs', 3 August 'Promiscuity', 5 October 'Parents'. Discussion started at 4.30pm while the group met at 3pm.

368   Ibid.

369   Jayson Mannings email to author, 9 February 2020.

370   Pen-Friend Scheme Details (PFS). Report by Jamie Styles, 26 January 1986 in Steve Lunniss's papers deposited in the Islington Local History Centre.

371   Clews (2017) pp90–91.

372   This was before the more well-known organisation Stonewall was formed. *Evening Standard*, 21 January 1985, report by Peter Hounam outlining a plan to open a hostel for gay and lesbians aged 17–25. The plan was opposed by Dr Andrew Crowcroft, who raised concerns about gay prostitutes using the hostel and mixing with older homosexuals. The hostel was to be for 10 people in a large house in Finsbury Park.

373   Press release, 4 October 1985. Steve Power's papers. In an email Steve Power to author, 1 October 2020, Steve explained how the name for the disco came about: 'My dad was working at Fords as an electrician and I think I thought of Alternator and Andy Chase turned it into Alternatre, something to do with new power'.

374   Martin Collins' message to author on Facebook, 17 October 2018. Steve Power says it was set up in June 1983 at his flat on the Gascoigne Estate (Steve Power email to author, 21 September 2019). Steve Power's papers include a letter he wrote 22 April 1983 to John Meredith from 55 Cobham House, St Margarets, Barking (Gascoigne Estate).

375   *Capital Gay*, 14 June 1985.

376   'Do gay boys just want to have fun?: Reflections on the London Gay Teenage Group 1985–1989' Anthony Hillin, Senior Youth Worker (unpublished) (2020).

377   Islington Local History Centre have a photo album of the LGTG (Islington Local Authority reference: S/IP/1) which includes photos taken on the Gay Pride marches in 1985 and 1986 with the LGTG banner being carried. The photo album also contains documents and photos from the David Harlech Democracy Award. The third-place certificate in the album lists Mike Sage, a pseudonym used by Michael Johnson, and Julian Withers (another pseudonym?). Others taking part of the production were Matthew Scudamore, Matthew C, Nine R, Wayne Brimmer, Brendon and Robert K. The script, a five-page document, is in Matthew Scudamore's papers in the LMA: London Gay Teenage Group, B20/050 (uncat).

378   *Lesbian and Gay Youth* issue 18, spring 1986.

379   Martin Collins comment on closed Facebook group, 10 August 2019.

380   Martin Collins comment on closed Facebook group, 14 August 2019.

381   Facebook communication 17 July 2019. The Keith Trotman referred to by Jon Pyper was a young white man who is not to be confused with another Keith Trotman who was mentioned in Chapter 8.

382   Author, Clifford Williams' recollections. In February 2014 Mark Dowd wrote to *The Guardian* and mentioned attending the NUS gay rights conference in Leeds in 1980. This may have been the same conference the author attended. Dowd commented 'One of the keynote speakers, who was allowed to address us uninterruptedly for more than half an hour, was a member of PIE. He claimed that pre-pubescent children were fully capable of giving full consent to sexual activity with adults. When I angrily asked the organisers what the PIE agenda had to do with the rights of adults like myself (still legally underage) to consent to same-sex behaviour, I was brushed off and told to mind my own business'. Guardian archives (Feb 2014) (following an article about PIE infiltrating the NCCL). Toby Keynes, e mail to author 1 June 2021, states he attended a NUS Gay Rights conference 2-4 Nov 1979. Were these the dates of the one the author attended in Leeds?

383   *Ealing Leader*, 5 September 1986, 'MP attacks schools gay phone plan'.

384   *White Lion Press*, 22 December 1986, a two-page article which includes some incorrect statements such as the LGTG receiving funding from ILEA in 1976 after a two-year battle. The battle was actually won in 1979.

385   HCA/CHE2/13/27 for flyer.

386   *Illustrated London News*, 1 December 1986, 'AIDS London's Last Chance'.

387   https://blog.nationalarchives.gov.uk/aids-health-campaign/ (accessed 13 August 2020).

388   There had been some public health campaigns before this big push e.g. Health Education Council AIDS advice leaflet, 1985.

389   *Public Health England: Trends in new HIV diagnoses and in people receiving HIV-related care in the United Kingdom: data to the end of December 2018.* Health Protection Report, 6 September (2019).

390   I am grateful to Jane Dixon who in 2019 provided me with copies of a number of documents. The Working Party letter, dated March 1986, invited members, workers and management committee members of lesbian and gay youth groups to attend the meetings on 5 April and 19 April 1986, at the LLGC in Cowcross Street, London WC 1.

391   Islington Area Youth Committee, 13 May 1986, minute 11.b LMA/
       ILEA/PS/AY005/04/01.

392   Islington Youth Office, December 1986, no name is given as to the
       author of the document.

393   Letter dated 7 July 1986, signed by 12 members of the South London
       Lesbian and Gay Young People's Group to ILEA. Signatures include
       K Trotman (chairperson), Barry E Lewis, Sandra Harman and Liam
       Curran. Copy of letter provided to author by Jane Dixon. A copy of this
       letter is also in LMA/ILEA/PS/AY005/04/01. K Trotman is the young
       Black man who worked in the late 1980s for Greenwich Lesbian and
       Gay Centre.

394   Petition letter dated 8 July 1986 signed by 14 people, mostly attenders
       at the LGTG, headed 'Age Restrictions on Lesbian and Gay Youth
       Groups', LMA/ILEA/PS/AY005/04/01.

395   'Working with young lesbians and young gay men in the youth service'
       by Jane Dixon, 22 October 1986. With cover note ILEA London Youth
       Committee Report by Principal Youth Officer 21 January 1987. CEC1
       10/87 Progress report of the Specialist Youth Officer for work with gay
       and lesbian young people (provided to author by Jane Dixon and now
       in Islington Local History Centre).

396   I believe this was actually the South London Lesbian and Gay Young
       People's Group, previously known as the South London Gay Young
       People's Group.

397   Letter John Broadbent HMI to Ms Jane Dixon (ILEA), 26 March 1987
       (provided to author by Jane Dixon and now in Islington Local History
       Centre).

398   *Daily Mail*, 14 March 1987.

399   *The Star*, 17 March 1987.

400   *The Sun*, 6 March 1987, 'Gays put Kinnock in panic'. *Daily Express*,
       6 March 1987, 'Kinnock admits: Lefties sank us'. *London Evening
       Standard*, 6 March 1987, 'New "loony" leaks feared by Labour'. *The
       Times*, 7 March 1987, 'Labour reels at "loony" left leak'.

401   Extract from letter Patricia Hewitt to Frank Dobson – leaked letter
       published by *The Sun*, 6 March 1987.

402   Jeffrey Weeks (2016) p239.

403   HCA/CHE2/12/39.

404   Bishopsgate Institute, LGBTM/234.

405   Ticket and poster in Bishopsgate Institute archives, LGBTM/147/16.

406   The First International Gay Youth Conference was Amsterdam in 1984. Bishopsgate Institute BL Oslo papers Switchboard, SB/10/2/2.

407   Gay Young London Group at 51 Argyle Street, London WC 1.

408   Young Black Lesbian Group in Peckham at 69 Bellenden Road, London SE 15.

409   NUS Lesbian and Gay Caucus at 461 Holloway Road, London N7.

410   Bishopsgate Institute archives, LGBTM/147/16.

411   Photo in *Tribune*, 21 August 1987, in LAGNA.

412   See Harris 1990: this was part of the ILEA programme that started in 1985 but folded in 1988.

413   The Prime Minister was sent highlighted extracts 'in order to obtain the flavour of this very disturbing book'. Letter 16 March 1987 to Parliamentary Private Secretary Michael Alison from Baroness Caroline Cox, TNA PREM19/4734. The entertainer Max Bygraves wrote a very different novel also called *The Milkman's on His Way* published in 1977!

414   James Byrne email to author, 25 August 2020.

415   'Do gay boys just want to have fun?: Reflections on the London Gay Teenage Group 1985–1989' Anthony Hillin, Senior Youth Worker (2020).

416   Telephone conversation, 18 August 2020. The woman in the other youth worker role would probably have been either Kim Nagle or Denise Worme.

417   Anthony Hillin (2020) op cit.

418   *Hansard*, House of Commons debate, 15 December 1987, vol 124 cc987–1038 extracts.

419   *Pink Paper* issue 8, 14 January 1988. Members of the LGTG also attended a march in April 1988 against the clause, as James Byrne recalled: 'I actually met my previous partner, James Papa, at a clause 28 march in London on 30 April 1988. I went along with others from the LGTG to protest. James was friends with some of the other members in the LGTG and we got talking. He moved in with me five days later and were together for eight years until his untimely tragic death. So, although clause 28 was terrible, I did get something great out of it that would not have happened otherwise. Life is strange' (email to author, 5 November 2020).

420   *Pink Paper* issue 13, 18 February 1988.

421   Education Legal Opinion to the Association of London Authorities, 36 Old Queen Street, London W1H 9JF, 22 June 1988, HCA/CHE2/12/3.

422   See Chapter Sixteen: 1990, when the grant was restored.

423   'Do gay boys just want to have fun?: Reflections on the London Gay Teenage Group 1985–1989' Anthony Hillin, Senior Youth Worker (2020).

424   James Byrne email to author, June 2020.

425   Ibid.

426   Anthony Hillin op cit.

427   Martin Collins on closed Facebook group, 10 August 2019.

428   North London Line Annual Report, 1988–89.

429   Ayo Brown, aka Ayodeji Oyebade, featured in a BBC news item, 1 July 2009: http://news.bbc.co.uk/local/london/hi/people_and_places/newsid_8128000/8128531.stm 'I was the token gay black man' (accessed 4 July 2021).

430   James Byrne email to Anthony Hillin, 30 June 2020. The Queen Mother was aged 87 at the time of the visit. She lived to 101 years.

431   *Capital Gay*, 28 July and 4 August 1989.

432   'Gay Youth and AIDS' by D A Feldman, pp185–193 in Herdt (1989).

433   Shaun Hanson message on Facebook to author, 3 July 2020.

434   Jayne County, a trans woman, born 1947 Dallas, USA, moved to London in 1977 and formed the band Wayne County and the Electric Chairs. When County moved to Berlin in 1979, she changed her stage name to Jayne County.

435   Report in *Metro: Magazine of the London Gay Teenage Group* issue 13 (Steve Power's papers).

436   *Pink Paper*, 15 April 1989. But the author understands that David is no longer alive.

437   *Pink Paper* issue 93, 7 October 1989.

438   *Pink Paper*, 4 November 1989.

439   *Gay Times* issue 146, November 1990.

440   *The Stage*, 25 January 1990, 'Gay play to get the go-ahead'.

441   Leaflet in Bishopsgate Institute archives, FL/EPH/C/673.

442   *Luton Herald and Post*, 21 February 1991, 'MP raps gay group backing'.

443   On 16 April 1992 at 1pm. Parliament was not sitting that day.

444   Notice in *Pink Paper*, 26 April 1992.

445   Richard Collumbell in closed Facebook group. Comment 9 August 2019 on post showing advert for Staying Out: Young L&G (teenage group). Meets in Hackney Tuesday evenings 7-10pm. Tel 081 986 5222 (Graham) Weekdays/Eves. Advert appeared in the *Pink Paper* 26 April 1992.

446   *Pink Paper* issue 223, 26 April 1992.

447   *Evening Standard*, 7 October 1992, 'The Prime Suspect: How Islington hindered a police investigation into a former worker, a boy in care and a pornographer'.

448   *Private Eye*, 30 May 1997, 'Rotten Boroughs'.

449   *Islington Gazette*, 3 July 2019, 'Islington child abuse scandal: Still no payouts for survivors two years on from council pledge'.

450   'Gay Youth 1993' part of Sandi Hughes' History of the Liverpool Scene 1975–2005. http://rewindfastforward.net/2017/06/27/gay-youth-1993/ (accessed 4 July 2021).

451   *OUT*, 9 August 1994. See also *Irish Independent*, 4 August 1994, 'TD furious as gays turn up for conference'.

452   The clause put forward by Edwina Currie to lower the age of consent for homosexual acts to 16 was defeated by 27 votes (Ayes 280, Noes 307). HC Deb, 21 February 1994.

453   *Sunday Telegraph*, 18 December 1994, 'My boy was lured away by gays and youth workers'.

454   *Pink Paper*, 14 April 1995, 'Youth Group wins section 28 fight'.

455   Richard Desmond e-communication to author, 29 October 2018.

456   *Pink Paper*, 14 June 1996, 'Lotto handout for gay youth'. Maureen Hand, who was working for the North London Line, went on to be the full-time youth worker for Freedom Youth based in Bristol.

457   *Pink Paper*, 26 January 1996, 'Gay teenager study breaks new ground'. No record of the outcome of her research during 1996–97 has been found by the author to date (October 2020). Sarah Cundy's 1994 Master of Philosophy dissertation was *Anti-Gay Violence and Discrimination: Challenging the Silence* (University of Cambridge).

458   *The Independent*, 22 March 1997.

459   Richard Collumbell message to author on Facebook, 27 January 2020.

460   Richard Collumbell to author, message on Facebook, 18 February 2019. The youth worker resigned after he had been sleeping with members and the council were cross with Richard because they thought he had fired the youth worker! In fact the youth worker had resigned as the committee were uncomfortable when a youth told them that the worker had slept with him. For a period the group operated without a youth worker.

461   *Stonewall Magazine* vol 6 no 2, September 1998. No copies of *Next Generation* have been found to date (July 2021).

462   Manor Gardens have not kept any records of the hiring of the hall that far back. There is no mention of the LGTG in the Manor Gardens Annual Report 2002, in which tenant organisations (40 charities and community groups) based at the centre then are listed, LMA/4314/04/094.

463   *Liverpool Echo*, 24 December 1998, p33.

464   In January 2021 Channel 4 released an equally powerful Russell T Davies drama, *It's a Sin*. Capturing the life of a group of young gay men in the period 1981–90, this drama portrayed the devastating effect of AIDS. The author found the five-part series excellent but also haunting.

465   *Gay News* issue 8, January 1977.

466   Chris Heaume email, 22 January 2020.

467   An interview with Chris Heaume by Lucy Delap in May 2012 is held by the British Library. BL C1667/08.

468   Emails Chris Heaume to author, 21 August 2018 and 4 June 2020. Originally Chris was given the part in *Nighthawks* of a good friend of the central character Jim, a teacher (played by Ken Robertson). Meeting up to go clubbing, and cruising separately, then coming back together from cruising periodically for a chat. The character ended up on the cutting-room floor. And then some of those cuts appeared in *Strip Jack Naked* (1991), a film in which Ron Peck talks about his experiences of growing up as a gay man, the attitudes to homosexuality in Britain, and his journey towards making his film *Nighthawks*.

469   Chris Heaume email to author, 13 August 2019.

470   Minutes of the SAYS and Gay Youth Workers Group are held in HCA/ Albany Trust/16/51.

471   HCA/Albany Trust/16/50. The first meeting of SAYS was held at the NAYC HQ.

472   *CHE Youth News* issue 6.

473   HCA/Albany Trust/16/50.

474   *Times Education Supplement*, 23 May 1980, 'Union probes sacking of gay youth leader'.

475   McMullen founded Streetwise in 1985. The committee governing Streetwise was chaired by Professor Donald West. Members in 1986 included LGTG ex-chair Steve Lunniss. The main object of the organisation was 'to promote the moral and social welfare and the preservation of the health of young persons who are, or are at risk of being, involved in prostitution in the Greater London Area, by

establishing, maintaining and developing a service in the Greater London Area and in particular in the London Borough of Kensington and Chelsea for the giving to such persons of individual and group counselling and practical advice' (constitution of Streetwise adopted 2 October 1986), Streetwise document (ring bound, 42 pages), November 1986 (Steve Lunniss's papers in Islington Local History Centre).

476 Reported on 'GayWaves' Radio, 7 July 1982, British Library C586/343.

477 Minutes of Gay Youth Work Group meeting, 13 September 1983. Mrs Denman was ILEA's equal opportunities officer at the time. Steve Power's papers.

478 *Capital Gay*, 18 November 1983.

479 Leaflet undated given to author from Jane Dixon. A set of minutes for a meeting held 9 May 1985 at the Venture Centre, Wornington Road, London W 10, of the Lesbian and Gay Youth Workers Group, are in LMA/ILEA/PS/AY005/04/21.

480 Leaflet given to author by Jane Dixon, placed in Islington Local History Centre.

481 Chris Heaume email to author, 3 October 2020.

482 Chris Heaume email to author, 8 September 2020.

INDEX

References preceded by *n* indicate endnote numbers: thus, '*Birmingham Post*, *n*12' denotes material at endnote 12 (on page 143).

Liberation Front)

Gay Life (TV series), 36, 63, *n*3, *n*150

Gay News: author discovers, xvi; on
Young Gays Conference (1972), 7;
on age of consent, 11; on CHE Young
Gays Conference (1975), 17; reports
homophobic attacks, 20; prosecuted
for blasphemous libel (1976), 43;
coverage of LGTG, 31, 33, 34, 48, 56,
80; LGTG advertises in, 40, 81; on Rose
Robertson, 4, 42–3; on setting up gay
youth groups, 60; on Manchester Gay
Youth Group, 79

gay police officers, 82–3, *n*301

Gay Sweatshop theatre company, *n*107,
*n*286

Gay Switchboard, 27, 46, 49, 73, 77, 109,
*n*259

Gay Teenagers Video Project (*later* Gay
Youth Video Project), *n*333

Gay Young London Group, 114

Gay Youth (magazine), 73–4, 75, 97, 109;
criticised, 99; becomes *Lesbian and Gay
Youth,* 101; last issue, 113

Gay Youth Movement (GYM): established,
47, 67; aims and objectives, 67;
anarchic structure, 122; number of
members, 75, 91, 92, 94; funding, 91–2;
summer camps, 70, 73, 82, 89, 91, 108,
113–14, *n*324, *n*333; workshops and
activist weekends, 71, 77, 91, 108;
penfriend scheme, 92, 94, 99–100;
phone line, 108; postbag, *n*339; *Gay
Youth* magazine, 73–4, 75, 97, 99, 101,
109, 113; London Conference (1980),
67; AGM at Durham GayFest (1981),
75; support for PIE and paedophilia,
75–6, 90, 97, 99; London Conference
(1982), 81–2; publishes Gay Youth
Charter, 82; speech at 1982 Labour
Party conference, 84; address to British
Youth Council, 86; lobbies Parliament
on age of consent, 86; 'GYM'LL Fix
It' event (1983), 87–8, 108; at Pride
events, 89, 100; Spring event (1984),
97; extreme stance, 97, 99, 100; at
demonstration in Rugby (1984), 101;
in crisis, 101; renamed Lesbian and Gay
Youth Movement (LGYM), 101; Spring
Festival (1985), 102; feud with LGTG,
107–8; demise, 114, 118, 122–3; impact
and legacy, 97, 109; Lyn Thomas's

recollections, 91–2

Gay Youth R Out (Liverpool), 132

Gay Youth Video Project (*later* Lesbian and
Gay Youth Video Project), 90, *n*333

Gay Youth Workers Group, 133–4

Gay's the Word (bookshop), 88, 102

GaySocs, 6–8, 74

Gaywaves pirate radio, 64, 82, *n*107

Giannaris, Connie, 90

Gibberd, Mike, 12

Gibbs, AN, 42

Gibbs, Robert, 37–8, 41

Gill, John: involvement in the LGTG, 22–3,
24, 26; collates material for *Offensive
Prose,* 23

Gleaves, Roger, 14–15, *n*68

Gleghorn, Paul, 82

GLF (Gay Liberation Front): Youth Group
(*later* Youth and Education Group), 4–5,
9, *n*23; campaigning, 5; divisions and
in-fighting, 6; influence and political
significance, 67; *see also Come Together;
names of individual groups*

Grant, John, 20

Grapevine, Holloway Road: location, xvi;
venue for early LGTG get-togethers, 27,
30, 31, 34, 50, *n*121; continued use of
premises by LGTG, *n*145; sex education
service, 33, *n*121; hosts Conference
on Young Gays (1978), 46–7; office
move, 51–2, 54; JCGT/GYM weekend
workshop, 71

Greater London Council (GLC): County
Hall, 40–1, 55, 91–2; Gay society, 24;
funding for LGTG, 85, 86, 92; 'Rates cash
for teenage gays' row, 92–3; 'loony left'
equalities policy, 89, 113; sponsorship
of LGTG research project, 106, 117;
Lesbian and Gay Charter, 106; pushback
against, 107; calls for abolition of, 89

Greater Manchester Youth Association, 37

Green, Richard, 127

Green, Sarah, 75

Greenway, Harry, 79, 109

Greenwich by-election (26 February
1987), 112–13

Gregor, Simon, 51

Grey, Antony, 1, 3, 14, 15, 16, 61

grooming, 19

Growing up homosexual (booklet), 6, 40

Guardian, The, 46, *n*382

Guild of Abstaining Youth (GAY), 1, *n*6

of ILEA youth committees, 42, 52, 55; application opposed, 42, 43, 52, 53, n170; legal position considered by ILEA, 43; application supported by Brook Advisory Centre, 44; notable members, 40; notable visitors, 43, 48–50, 125; upstaged by PIE at NAYC conference, 44–5; at Conference on Young Gays (1978), 46; and JCGT, 47, n180; seeks new premises, 48, 51–2, n186; threat of prosecution against, 51, 52, n200; moves to Manor Gardens in Islington, 54–5, 56; Young Lesbian Group established, 56; wins recognition from ILEA, 56, 58, n211; day-to-day running of the group, 58; compared with Gay Youth Movement, 67; breakaway of Young Lesbian Group, 78; youth worker post advertised, 78; row over ILEA funding, 78–9; Gregg Blachford appointed, 79–80, 81; Gaywaves broadcast (July 1982), 82; Amsterdam rent boy incident (1982), 84; awarded grants by GLC, 85, 86, 92; response to Thompson Report, 85; commissions research, 86; 'Rates cash for teenage gays' row, 92–3; group renamed, 102, 107, 132, n362; 10th anniversary party, 107; feud with LGYM, 107–8; petitions ILEA over minimum age policy, 111; mentioned in Parliament, 89, 95, 117–18; opposes section 28, 119; effect of section 28 on running of group, 119–20; appearance on *Network 7*, 123; youth worker resignation incident, 132, n460; final years a mystery, 132; possibly superseded, 131; reunion picnic (2019), 141; impact and legacy, 109, 124

running the group: advertisements, 31, 33, 40; age group policy, 40, 53, 74, 76–7, 81, 84, 110–11, 115, n264; AGMs, 76–7, 92, 100, 109; aims and objectives of group, 54, 81; Annual General Report (1982), 81; attendance, 81, 98; badges and badge making, 51, 87; cliqueyness, 46; complaints from parents, n264; constitution, 76–7, 81, 92; counselling and giving support, 121–2, 124; equipment, 70; excursions and trips, xvi, 34, 43, 53–4, 62, 64, 84–5; finances, 30, 40, 51, 55, 60, 65–6, n241; fundraising, 32, 51, 65, 70, 83–4,

94, 96–7, 132; gay politics and social education, 80, n286; general committee, 31, 54, 58; grants and payments, 55, 60, 65–6, 79, 85, 86, 92, 98, n241; group composition, 44, 122; lesbian members, xvi, 52, 56, 102, 107, 109; loud 'screaming queen' issue, 53, 70–1, 76, 80, 84, 95; management committee, 56–8, 77, 81, 92, n296; number of members, 81, 98; over-21s at, 40, 76, 81, n294; participation, 81; pen pal scheme, 32, 40, 54, 105–6; predatory sexual environment, 38–9, n155, n264; at Pride events, 89, 100, n377; publicity, 33, 40, 63, 75, 77, 84; referrals to, 81; as refuge from commercial gay scene, 54, 63; rent boys at, 84, n313; research committee, 86; residential weekends, 115–16, 121, 124; safeguarding practices, 38; safer sex education, 121, 124; social events, 34, 40, 48–9, 52, 63–4; Sponsorship Scheme, 70, n253; talks to youth clubs, 35–6, 88; telephone helpline and training, 30, 69, 75, 120; transformative power of, 124; under-16s at, 74, 84, 110–11, 115, 125, n264; vetting of new members, 37–8; welcoming new people to the group, 104; youth worker support, 58, 65, 95, 102–3, n367

publications: 'The London Gay Teenage Group – a report after the first six months' (July 1977), 34, n145; *Metro* (magazine), 24, 45–6, 58, n363; *Next Generation* (magazine), 132, n461; *Pink Gym* (magazine), 69, n252; *SNU, The* (magazine), n363; *Something to tell you,* 94–5, 104, 106, 117; *Talking about School,* 100; *Talking about Young Lesbians,* 100; *Talking about Youth Work,* 100, 135; *Visions* (magazine), 102, n364

recollections of members: Marc Burke, 82–3; James Byrne, 115, 120–1, 123; Josef Cabey, 95–6; Martin Collins, 59–60, 65–6, 69–70; Richard Collumbell, 132; Michael Connew, 38–9, 49–50; Richard Desmond, 71; Thomas Flanagan, 61; Shaun Hanson, 125; Ash Kotak, 71–3; Steve Lunniss, 96–7; Jayson Mannings, 105; Kevin O'Neill, 64; Owen, 80; Steve Power, 25–6, 27,

National Association of Youth Clubs (NAYC): recommends *Growing up homosexual,* 6; Birmingham conference (1976), 23; support for gay issues, 134; Sheffield conference (1978), 44–5; Keith Andrews elected, 61; Hull conference (1980), 61, 65, *n*239; donation to Gay Youth Movement, 67; Warwick conference (1982), 82; Nottingham conference (1984), 100

National Council for Civil Liberties (NCCL), 20, 134

National Council for Voluntary Youth Service, 15–16, 28

National Lottery funding, 131

National Organisation of Lesbian and Gay Youth and Community Workers (NOLGYCW), 135

National Union of School Students, 7, 12, 47

National Union of Students (NUS): gay rights policy, 7–8, 9; invited onto JCGT, 47; Gay Rights conference (1979–80), 109, *n*382; far-left politics, 109; Lesbian and Gay Caucus, 114

National Youth Bureau, 33, 133

Nationwide Festival of Light, 53, 78–9, *n*170; *see also* Whitehouse, Mary

NAYPCAS (National Association of Young People's Counselling and Advisory Services), 22

NCCL *see* National Council for Civil Liberties

Nelson, Anthony, 53–4

Network 7 (TV programme), 123

New Horizons, 15

Newcastle Evening Chronicle, 90

Newcastle Friend, 89

Next Generation (magazine), 132, *n*461

Nighthawks (film), 133, *n*468

Nightline (radio show), 83

Nilsen, Denis, 87

Norcross, Lawrie, 78

North Devon: LGYM summer camp (1986), 113

North London Line (lesbian and gay youth project), 74, 115, 123, 126

North London Young Lesbian Group *see* Young Lesbian Group (YLG)

North-Western Homosexual Law Reform Committee (NWHLRC), 8

North Westminster Detached Youth Project, 46

Northern Theatre Company, Hull, 127

Notting Hill Lesbian and Gay Youth Group, 119, 127

Novac, Andrew, 15

Nucleus (community welfare organisation), 16

Observer, The, 4, 51

O'Carroll, Tom, 44–5

O'Connor, Pat, 17

Offensive Prose (poetry book), 23, *n*106

O'Grady, Paul, 10

O'Neill, Kevin: at West Mersea youth camp, 64; open letter to members of the LGTG, 70–1

Orme, Dr J (of Sheffield), 3

Orrill, Sam, 12

Out (book), 73

OUT (TV programme), 130

'Out on Thursday' (gay youth group), 126

Outrage! (campaigning group), 130

Oval House theatre and cafe, Kennington, 16, 24, 26, 56, *n*108, *n*110, *n*333

Ovenden, Mark, 83

Owen (LGTG member), 80, *n*289

Oyebade, Ayo *see* Brown, Ayo

Oz obscenity trial (1971), 9

PACE (Project for Advice, Counselling and Education), 103, 131

Paddick, Brian, xv

paedophilia, 19–20, 75–6; *see also* PIE

Palmer, Dr Paulina, 46

Papa, James, *n*419

Parents Enquiry: origins, 4; operations and services, 4, 43, 51; CHE urges support for, 11, 17; lesbian callers, 42–3; legal concerns dealing with under-21s, 43; at Conference on Young Gays (1978), 46; and JCGT, 47; LGTG decides not to affiliate with, 53; contact details publicised, 68, 89

Parker, Jan, 88

Peacock, Mari *see* Johnson, Michael

Peck, Ron, 133, *n*468

Peckham Young Black Lesbian Group, 114

Perry, Glen, 59, *n*239

Philip (LGTG member), 52

Piccadilly boy prostitution racket, 15

Piccadilly Circus Station, 59, 84

Pickles, Veronica, 12

27; early get-togethers at Oval House, 26; GLC Gay society, 24; en route to CHE Annual Conference, 23; relationship with Philip Cox, 24, *n*109; elected LGTG treasurer, 31; leaves group, 29, 31; involvement with CHE Young London, 31

West, Professor Donald, *n*475

West Mersea youth camp, 64

West Midlands Gay Switchboard, 47

Wester, Dennis, 133

Westminster child sex abuse inquiry, 19–20, *n*93

White, Ian A, 130

White, Tony, 15

White Report (1995), 130

Whitehouse, Mary, 46, 52, *n*200; *see also* Nationwide Festival of Light

Whitton, Rev Eric, 15

Wilenius, Fred, 133

Wilkinson, Graham, 12

Wilkinson, Sarah, *n*296

Williams, Alan, 45–6, 57

Williams, Clifford: schooldays, xv; discovers *Gay News,* xvi; first visit to the LGTG, xvi; in LGTG football team, *n*188; Radio London talk show, 49; analyses JCGT survey, 66; at NUS Gay Rights conference (1979–80), 109, *n*382; at Carved Red Lion disco, 74–5; ruse to attend NAYC conference in Hull, *n*239; recollections of the LGTG, xvi–xvii, 44, 49, 53–4, 64, *n*201; researches history of the group, xvii–xviii; gives talks on the LGTG, xviii

Williams, Judith, 135

Williams, Kenneth, 88

Williams, Paul, *n*296

Willis, Martin, 32, *n*137

Winn, Mr Justice, 2

Withers, Julian, 107, *n*377

Wolverhampton CHE group, 2

Wolverhampton Express and Star, 1

Woman's Hour, 56

Wood, Deirdre, 113

Workman, Bob, 33, *n*142

Worme, Denise, *n*416

Wylie, Thomas, 15

Yelland, Graham, 100

Young, Sir George, 89

Young Gay Women and Men Group (East London), 106

Young Lesbian Group (YLG): established, 56; breaks away from LGTG, 78; volunteer youth worker support, 86, 98; row over ILEA funding for gay youth groups, 78–9; summer camp at Ingleton (1984), 98

Youth News, 22, 23, 24

youth rights advocacy, 108–9

youth workers, gay and lesbian *see* gay and lesbian youth workers

Zold, John, 69